Divine Interventions
True stories about God's miracles
LS King

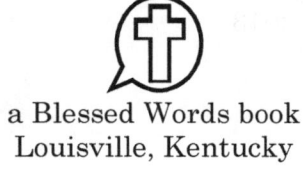

a Blessed Words book
Louisville, Kentucky

DIVINE INTERVENTIONS

Copyright ©2012, 2013 by LS King

All rights reserved, including the right to reproduce this book, or portion thereof, in any form. Written permission must be secured from the publisher to use or reproduce any part of this book, except for brief quotations in critical reviews or articles.

A Blessed Words Book
Blessed Words Publishing
10307 Chimney Ridge Ct, Louisville, KY 40299

Printed in the United States of America.

ISBN: 978-1-61318-123-2
LCCN: 2011944766
Cover design by Dave Mattingly
Cover photo by Tim Wood, Orange Beach, AL
Edited by Linda Mattingly

First Edition: January 2012
Second Edition: April 2013

Foreword

Love.

When we think of love we usually think of hearts, flowers, kisses and a picture of the person, or persons, that mean the most to us. Right down to the family pet. Seldom do we picture the unconditional love that Christ has for us. We pray for love, we search for love and we use the word freely to speak of objects that we are happy to have or wish to obtain. For example: "I love that dress." "I loved your dinner." "I loved that movie."

Love is one of the most used words in the dictionary. When we want to overemphasize our feelings, love just jumps out of our mouth. I always tell my children that I love them before I hang up the phone or as they leave my house. In this moment love has a strong meaning in my heart and in my mind. It is different from the love I have for my new shoes.

Have you ever linked love to the interventions in your life? Could love save you from a near death accident? Can love be the reason your cancer has suddenly disappeared? Can love be the reason bad things happen to you? Can love be the reason you are placed in your job? Can love be the reason you gravitated to your best friend?

It is my opinion that God's love puts you where you are today. If you are not happy with your life, then maybe you are not following God's plan for your life. Maybe you don't believe.

In this book, hopefully you will see **"Love"** is so many things but the most exciting love is that love that teaches, saves us, and gives us knowledge. It's the love we will truly understand once we develop a relationship with God who is in control of everything that happens to his believers. Even death and tragedy.

1 Corinthians 2:9-11

However it is written, No eye has seen, No ear has heard, no mind has conceived what God has prepared for those who love him, but God has revealed it to us by his spirit. The spirit searches all things, even the deep things of God. For who among men knows the thoughts of a man, except the man's spirit within him? In the same way, no one knows the thoughts of God except the Spirit of God.

The man without the spirit of God does not understand God. God's love and ways are foolish to the unbeliever.

I pray that you don't put this book down now because you may not agree whit the Bible. Keep an open mind and enjoy the stories and maybe you can understand why I felt the importance to write about divine interventions.

Try to set your mind on the things above and not on the things that are here on earth. Remember that love is the main reason God brings interventions to us here on earth. I challenge you to share this book with someone you love.

Introduction

It was Christmas and I had several items in my basket waiting with others at the checkout counter. A young girl named Sheila was carefully placing my purchases in a bag. I could tell that her mind was not on the tags she was scanning.

"Are you ready for Christmas?" I asked.

She replied, "No not really. I don't have enough money to buy Christmas for my children this year. I am raising three children by myself. I have to work two jobs to pay the bills. I don't care if I get anything for Christmas, but I hate to see the children disappointed."

"I understand your concern. The economy is bad for everyone right now," I replied.

She smiled, handed me my bag and wished me a Merry Christmas.

I really didn't understand. I had never been in a situation where I had to provide for three children by myself.

I thought about Sheila the rest of the day. If only I could help her in some way. I prayed for this girl and her family as I pulled out of the parking lot into the busy traffic. I felt blessed that I had money for Christmas plus money to buy myself an outfit for Christmas parties.

Then I prayed.

"Lord, if it is your will for me to help this family, show me what I need to do."

Later that week, I drove up to my mailbox and found an unexpected check from an investment that my husband and I receive monthly. Looking at it I realized it was the end of the year bonus check that was interest on money. It was such a surprise.

I bragged about the check to my family and friends.

"Now I have extra money to spend on Christmas gifts," I told my husband.

My mind was going wild. I bought all of my favorite things and invited my girlfriends over to have a party like Oprah where I would give away my favorite things. These were just goofy things like, gum, coke in a small bottle, foot spa cream, soap, hand cream and a few more.

Later that day I remembered the young girl behind the counter. The money was eating at me. I thought about my promise to God. Should I give money to this stranger? She seemed so sad. *Is this what God would do?* I silently asked. The face of the salesgirl haunted me. I tried to justify not returning to the store. Someone will help her, I said to myself. She is not my responsibility. Two days passed and I would hear about an angel tree or pass a Salvation Army person ringing a bell. It would haunt me and I would start thinking about the young girl. What if the role was reversed and I had children who would be skipping Christmas? Yes, I would be excited that someone gave me money. Is it the right thing to do? Without a doubt, I knew the answer to that question. Just to be on the safe side I procrastinated and confided in a Christian friend. She assured me that God was going to use me to supply Christmas for these children.

Without another thought, I went directly to the store and did what God was asking me to do.

I didn't even stop to get lunch. The closer I got to the store the more anxious I became. What if the young woman wasn't there? Then what should I do?

I walked into the store and asked to see Sheila. The young girl was in the back of the store. When she heard her name paged from the checkout counter, she walked over to her colleague. I could tell by the look on her face that she thought she was in trouble.

Surprisingly I immediately recognized the young girl.

"Take this and buy your children something for Christmas," I instructed. She clearly did not recognize me, but she started to cry. She opened the envelope and saw the large bills.

"Are you sure you have the right person?" she asked.

"Yes, I am." I replied. "You have three children don't you?"

Looking forlorn, she replied, "Yes I do, but how, why, who told you?"

"Just remember God loves you and he wants you to have this," I instructed.

"Thank you ma'am, you do not know how much I need this. How can I repay you?"

"It's a gift. Go shopping for the children," I replied.

I walked away and never saw her again.

Message from the Author

Do you believe that this was a divine intervention? What caused me to be in the store at the time this girl was working at the checkout counter? Did God place me there? How could it be that the bonus check would arrive the same week?

So many times we do not stop to count our blessings. I would like to think that this book will provide me an opportunity to do just that. Not only will I be counting my blessings, maybe you will identify with each situation and remember some of your blessings. There are so many subjects I could choose to write about. I have several subjects on the back burner. However, the divine interventions in my life are haunting me. Even some of my close friends have never heard how God has been a big part of who I am and why I believe.

Isn't it ironic how quickly we get on with our lives after we have been given a gift of healing or receive a piece of wonderful news that we have been praying about for months. We bask in the moment and then in a fleeting instant we are on to the next event complaining how unfair things seem to be. Do we just forget? Forget that we just experienced a miracle three months ago. Forget we were saved from a dreadful illness. Forget that someone paid the money they owed right before Christmas.

It's not just the big events we should be celebrating. I believe we should also remember the small things that we are unexpectedly awarded. Recently I heard someone on television talking about happiness. He explained that things only make us happy for a short time. It's the events in our life that we remember when we reminisce about a birthday party, childhood event, or a past Christmas.

I was a schoolteacher for years. I remember many children, but the children I remember the most are the ones that were a handful in class. The class clown, the child that tells amusing stories at show and tell, and the child who was always taking risks. I must admit I have to smile when I think about some of the kids and wonder where they are today. Did I make a difference in their lives? Was I an intervention? Was God using me to make an impression on a small child? I only know of one who claims that because of my attempt to make him feel special, he started believing in himself.

His name was Jamie. He was hydrocephalic and in my afternoon kindergarten class back in the seventies. When we had circle time I remember letting him sit next to me and I always validated any questions or answers he contributed to the class. I didn't realize that he was telling everyone that I was his favorite teacher until several years later.

Jamie's great aunt was a friend. She later told me that her nephew was in my kindergarten class and was always telling stories about school and his kindergarten teacher. When she learned that he was going into the army she called and told me about Jamie. His wife and mother invited me to his going away party. I showed up at the party and surprised him. I had no idea that he had bonded with me that much in school. He had no health problems. After several operations, I could not tell that he once looked different from others in the class. He was a wonderful father, spouse and now he was looking forward to serving his country. Isn't it amazing the way we can make a difference because God uses us as interventions in situations that change someone or something in life?

While reading this book, decide what you believe about miracles and divine interventions. Maybe you can recall several different events that will encourage you to think about your purpose in life. God has a plan for each of us. I have followed several paths, but I am still looking for what is around the corner. What is next for me? I can't really say, but I do enjoy writing, sharing with others and being creative. If God uses me I will feel blessed.

Thank you for choosing to read this book. You might not always believe in my theories behind divine interventions. I anticipate that you will read this book and relate to the many stories I have shared. It is my goal that whomever reads this will discuss the contents with others and share intervention stories. Keep a log of past events and a list of people who have been placed in your life. It's amazing to see the connections that bring people into our inter circle and how each situation changes us as individuals.

This book is excellent for book clubs and group discussions. Make notes as you read. Share with your group. Most of all, "MAKE A DIFFERENCE IN SOMEONE'S LIFE!"

Unexplainable Events? God's Plan

I am not a fortune teller. I don't read minds, and I don't claim to have any special powers. I just know when the Holy Spirit speaks to my heart and continues to direct me toward people and events. I pray about it and soon I find answers. Somehow, whatever action I decide to take feels like the right thing to push forward and do. I am endeavoring to be guided in my daily life by Jesus Christ through the Holy Spirit. He is my divine when I speak of divine interventions.

You may not believe in God. You may worship someone or something different. I respect your belief and I hope you will give me the same respect as you read this book and experience with me unexplained events that have taken place in my life. Things that I have witnessed personally. We all experience unexplainable events in our lives. This is how I explain the force behind these events. Your explanation may differ.

God had a plan for my life. In his plan, he designed a way for me to grow and learn what he wanted me to know about the world around me.

I believe that before we are even born, God designed us to accept his will. Given a will to learn, we (unique individuals) find out why and how things work. We desire to know about certain things in life. We all develop certain interest in the world that surrounds us. It is my opinion that God gives every person this desire to learn about certain things when he creates us in our mother's womb. The amazing science that decoded our DNA proves that no two people are alike. This supports my theory that God planned my life. It is amazing that we would learn what he wanted us to learn as we grow to adulthood. He gave us several years of learning from the time we are born, until the day we breath our last breath. There are so many twists and turns in life, like a train going around a mountain. Just when the track seems to be holding steady, a surprise takes us off to places undiscovered, and events that are unexpected. This is what I call interventions. Only God knows what is ahead of us in the future. (Most of the time, we are able to handle difficult situations with this unexpected circumstance because God has already prepared us mentally, physically, and emotionally.) If we find that we are not prepared, God gives us events, people, and answers that will open doors to learn new ways to handle difficult situations. I call it a divine intervention. What we learn previously allows us to solve problems with unexpected events. These unexpected events are learning experiences placed there by God.

In this book, I define adventures as learning experiences that may or may not be exciting. These experiences help in learning more about the environment around us. We (children of God) learn what works and what doesn't. Just like monkeys and rats studied in a laboratory, we quickly learn negative experiences that are unpleasant to our bodies. Knowing that we are not God, and therefore not perfect, we will mess up at times and repeat a negative experience. God will then send messages that will send unpleasant activities and thoughts to our brains. We eventually learn that this is not rewarding. Therefore, we change those activities that are not pleasant to a positive enjoyable experience. We are then rewarded with a positive response.

Unlike animals, God gives humans a conscience. So what is a conscience? A conscience is a feeling of uneasiness, that nags at our feelings when we do something that we learn is wrong through experiences. It can physically cause us to become sick. Again I reinforce that a conscience is a learned behavior. Notice that a baby does not have a conscience when it is born. They learn from adults that what they do is right or wrong. It may be a smack on the hand, or a specific sound like "NO." But, whatever it may be the child learns what is right or wrong. The child will eventually show remorse. Animals do not show remorse because they do not have a conscience. This is what makes us different from other animals.

Isn't it wonderful the way God works? He never promises that it is going to be easy. He does promise us that He will be there to help us through the adventure so we can become consistent with his word and learn what He wants us to know. It takes several falls for a baby to learn to walk, yet in God's time it will happen and soon the baby will learn that it is faster and easier to walk instead of crawl. The activity of crawling will digress as the fast pace of walking dominates the movement from one place to another to obtain the desires of the infant. True believers resemble the infant.

The curious thing about this promise is that some people never understand that God has a plan for each of us. Instead of infants people are like young children who beg for toys in a store hoping that the adults in their lives will give them what *they* want, not what they need. Some people never stop begging. Instead, they start blaming God because he just does not listen to their wants or prayers. In conclusion, unfaithful followers declare that in their life adventures, God never gives them what they want and God never answers their prayers. Why then should these people pray and ask God for help in time of need? Why pray at all?

If you believe that God does not hear your prayers then obviously you are not listening or remembering the pleasant experiences that you enjoyed when God rewarded you for good behavior. Your conscience will allow you to feel good about yourself. He is faithful and he will do as he has promised if we obey his word. Everyone has done something good in his or her lifetime. If this is true, the act of kindness rewarded a pleasant response. It only makes sense that if we were given praise for doing good things, then we should remember to repeat that positive behavior.

So why do unexplainable things happen in one's life? Could it be that God put you in the right place at the right time? Is there someone he wants you to meet or something that he wants you to learn? Is your life planned according to *His* time, or is it by chance?

In this book, you will read about true circumstances that happened to me, and people in my life who just happened to experience an intervention in life's adventures. You may ask yourself, "How can this be true?" I will tell you that everything I have written is true and I believe that God has planned each episode according to His will. For I believe that nothing is impossible with God.

Prayer Changes Things: The Story of Vickie and Matthew

The year was 1954. Vickie and Matthew had been married for fourteen years. It had not been a Godly marriage but they had one daughter who was nine years old and was desperately begging for a little sister of her own. Vickie grew up in a Christian home. She knew what God expected of her as a believer. She had sat through many a sermon conducted by her father. Vickie was reminded daily of what was right and what was wrong. Vickie did not have to refer to the gospel written in the Bible. It would be her father's gospel that she was most concerned about following.

When Vickie fell in love with Matthew, she knew right away that he was not a Christian. She knew that he did not know the Lord and would not be willing to share in her Christian life style. It did not matter to Vickie. She fell in love. Being in love was more important than waiting for God to send her a husband who had the same Godly values that she had. Honestly, she was getting a little tired of her restrictions given her, because she was the minister's daughter.

There was something exciting about a secret kiss here and there and a runaway Sunday afternoon without the whole town watching her actions. Following her heart, she pushed aside the morals of her childhood and married the love of her life. There was no way she could have known that he would turn out to be an alcoholic. Life could not be more difficult for Vickie. She prayed for the nights that he would stay home and give her the attention she wanted and needed as a wife. She did all the things she knew to make life wonderful for her husband. They did not have much money, but she could cook and learned how to can fresh fruits and vegetables to save money. She loved her home and her little girl. Matthew loved his little girl and Vickie. But the poison had a hold on his life. Along with the liquid he craved, came a woman who provided the companionship and encouragement he needed to continue his habit.

Vickie found out about the affair that Matthew was having at the local bar. She knew God was not in her life and down deep in her heart, she craved to see Matthew accept Christ in his life. After crying night after night and praying for changes, she realized that she was partly the blame for Matthew's behavior. She had never encouraged him to attend church or read Gods word.

Vickie would skip church on Sunday to take her daughter to the country to go fishing with Matthew. She longed for the weekends when it was spring and summer and the right time for fishing. Vickie knew Matthew would not drink when he took them to the country to spend time with Matthew's family. Matthew loved his family and for almost a year Vickie convinced Matthew that the only way they could have a family was to stop drinking and stop seeing the girl at work who was his drinking companion.

Vickie was willing to forgive Matthew if he would change jobs and stop drinking. It seemed that Vickie's prayers were answered. Matthew opened his own handy shop and spent every day along with Saturdays working to support his little family. He even joined the girls on trips to visit Vickie's family where he would have to attend church on Sundays. Matthew attended church and was baptized accepting Christ as his Savior. Vickie's family was happy to see the changes in his attitude. Still baptism was not the total package of Christianity. It was a big step for Matthew. Vickie was pleased. But he really didn't understand that giving your life to Christ was supposed to be a life-changing experience. Matthew still had the desire to drink and enjoy the company of other women. He was able to abstain for months, but soon the desires of his heart were longing to sin.

Having another child seemed to be the answer to solving the family problem. Vickie wanted a little brother or sister for her daughter Jill. It was all Jill could talk about at home and school. Silently Vickie knew that Matthew was not going to be supportive. However, maybe just maybe it would be an answer to prayer. Matthew would fall in love with another child and this would bring him back to her. He was beginning to spend more time away from home. He claimed that work was keeping him busy although the money was not increasing. Vickie did not want to believe that Matthew was returning to his old habits.

One evening after supper, Vickie asked Matthew to join her in the swing on the porch. She had noticed that Matthew was avoiding the porch. He was parking his car in the back of the house and again, his behavior was changing. With much persuading from Jill, Matthew gave in and joined the family out front. Carefully he watched as cars passed the house. He would slide down in the swing so he could not be seen by cars that passed by. Blocked by the wall of the porch and flower boxes, Matthew hoped that no one would see him there with his family.

Jill sat upon Matthew's lap.

"Jill tell Daddy what you want for your birthday," said Vickie.

"What's that Jill?" replied Matthew.

"A baby sister," answered Jill.

Matthew knew that having family was the most important thing that a person could possess. He had lost his parents at a young age. He was just thirteen years old when he went to live with an older sister in the city. He had never had limits and no one told him he was wrong. He knew he was missing something in his life, but no matter what he tried, he was never able to fill the emptiness he had when he lost his home. He wanted Jill to be happy with a real family. Even though he struggled with the influence of alcohol, he knew that he did not want to lose Jill and Vickie. He talked to Vickie that night and she made him feel good about his changed behavior and he promised to put things back in perceptive.

"Maybe a baby is what we need," said Matthew.

"A boy this time," encouraged Vickie.

"Maybe, but what will Jill do if she doesn't get that baby sister?" replied Matthew.

That night was the beginning of a magic time for Vickie and Matthew. Vickie got pregnant and in October of 1953, Vickie had a little girl. Matthew was not disappointed that he did not get his boy because he wanted Jill to be happy. Jill had already told everyone in her class that she was going to have a baby sister. Thank God, it was a baby girl. How would Vickie explain the appearance of a baby boy? Jill told Matthew and Vickie if the baby was a boy, they could just take it back to the hospital and exchange it for a sister.

For one year, Matthew was sober, working, and living at home. Then one day Vickie got a call from a woman who introduced herself as Matthew's girlfriend.

"Now that you and Matthew are separated," she announced, "Matthew and I are dating and we plan to get married when you give him a divorce," she warned.

Vickie found out that Matthew was telling her that he was separated from Vickie and living with his sister. She listened to all the lies and then she invited her to come over and look in Matthew's closet.

"Matthew has never left our house. He is living here and we are still married. That does not give you permission to date my husband," said Vickie.

She found out that fishing trips were trips taken with this so-called girlfriend. Vickie was furious. That night, she was going to confront Matthew with the news. It was time for him to arrive home. Vickie still upset with Matthew picked up her baby to put her in the highchair. At this point Vickie noticed her baby was having trouble breathing.

When Matthew came in the door, Vickie was leaving for the hospital with the baby. Matthew picked up Jill and took her next door to stay with the neighbor. Then he rushed Vickie and the baby to the hospital. On the way to the hospital, the baby was limp and semi-responsive. It was quiet and Vickie held the baby close to her broken heart praying that God would take care of everything.

Vickie and Matthew ran into the emergency room and the nurses took the baby out of Vickie's arms. Then she placed the baby under an oxygen tent. Two doctors rushed into the room and ordered x-rays for the baby. An hour later, one of the doctors came out to the waiting room and announced his plan to give her oxygen and an emergency tracheotomy.

"There is something wrong with her lungs. I hope she can make it but she is very weak and having a hard time breathing. We are going to take her into the operating room and try to open an airway," said the Doctor.

At this point Matthew fainted. The nurses were standing over Matthew as Vickie rushed behind the doctor to find the proper waiting room closest to her baby daughter. As the doctor approached the operating room door, he showed Vickie where to wait until the procedure was finished.

It seemed like everything was taking so long. Vickie looked around the room and wanted to find a phone to call her family. Instead, she saw another mother sitting by herself looking out a window.

Vickie wanted to pray. She needed to pray. If she could not call her parents, she would find the chapel and pray by herself. Suddenly she saw Matthew coming down the hall. He looked forlorn and lost. Vickie told him what was going on and then she turned to the mother sitting by herself and asked if she knew where the chapel was located. Pointing to the door across the hall, Vickie went swiftly to the chapel and told Matthew to come for her if the doctor came out of the operating room.

Vickie opened up the door and saw the statue of Mother Mary in front of the Catholic chapel. She quickly walked down the aisle toward the statue of Mary. Kneeling at the foot of the statue on a kneeling pad, she began to pray.

"Oh God, please hear my prayer. I know that I have not been listening to you. I have been listening to my heart. Forgive me for not being the Christian that I know I should be." Continuing with her prayer, Vickie closed her eyes and blocked out the sounds of the busy hallway.

"Please Lord, I pray that your will be done in my life. Please save my baby and I promise that I will take time to do what you want me to do. I promise I'll go back to church. Lord, I love Matthew but I know that he may not be in my life. Show me what to do Lord. I promise that I will go back to church, work in the church and be the Christian that I need to be."

At this point, Vickie felt a peace in her body that she had not had in years. She stared at the statue of Mary and then walked out of the chapel. Across the hall, Matthew was sitting on a couch still pale from the lack of blood flow to his head. She wanted to tell him about the phone call from his girlfriend, but this was not the time to start a verbal fight.

Matthew tried to comfort Vickie, but she moved to the door and stood lifeless waiting on an answer from the doctors and nurses that were in the operating room. Matthew was worried. If he planned to tell Vickie that he was leaving her, this was not the time. Instead, he was worried to death about his baby girl.

The door opened and the doctor came into the waiting room. He was smiling.

"I can't believe what we found," he said.

"The baby's x-rays show that she had a blockage in her lung. Just as we started to do a tracheotomy, the radiologist suggested that we first try to see if we could remove the object lodged in her lung. Looking at the picture, we noticed that it looked like the baby had ingested a safety pen. We put the baby to sleep and used our suction to pull out anything that might be loose in the lung. She continued to struggle with her breathing. To our amazement, we found that there was a clump of baby food in her right lung. It was a miracle. We did not have to open the lung or operate. I cannot explain it. She just stopped breathing long enough for us to suck the mass out of her lung. We thought we lost her there for a minute, but after the suction she started breathing on her own," explained the doctor.

Vickie knew it was a miracle. She did what she promised God. She put Him first in her life. From that day on, she attended church and took her two girls with her. Matthew continued to drink and eventually left Vickie for his love of drink and women. Vickie knew that God had given her a sign that He is real. She knew now that God had answered her prayers. When you seek answers from God, it may not be the way you want God to answer your prayer. In the grand scheme of things, God is in control and this was the first miracle that I know God answered in my life. I was the baby and God saved me to tell this story.

Believe That God is in Control: A Miracle for a Rabbit?

We must listen to the spirit connection in life. It assures us that God exists and he is sometimes mysterious. Most of all, he is awesome. I believe that God gives us simple ways to communicate with him. It may be a person, an event, or a chance meeting. It may be impossible to believe, because it is against all odds. At the right time in life, God will give you an opportunity to share your miracle. As I stated before, God has a larger plan for our lives. Sometimes we just do not understand until we experience the "I told you so moment" where a bell goes off in our heads and we realize it was a God thing. The Bible tells us that he will guide and protect you until you stand in his presence. Once we accept Christ in our life, it is impossible to separate yourself from him. He is always there. Just look for ways to communicate with him.

I have always had a connection with God. Somehow, without anyone explaining God's purpose in my life or learning facts in the Bible, I always knew that God could do anything. I suppose it was the years of church and Sunday school in the Methodist Church. Here I learned what my teachers and ministers wanted me to know. I never really searched or studied the Word on my own.

The second time I experienced a divine intervention was when I was about nine or ten years old.

Every Easter my mother would give me a real rabbit for Easter. They were usually small and still willing to nurse from a baby bottle. I would wrap it in a blanket and feed it like a baby.

One day while playing with my rabbit, in the kitchen floor, the rabbit just stopped walking and flopped over on its side.

I screamed, "My rabbit just died!"

My sister, who was ironing clothes between the dining room and kitchen door, fell to her knees and picked up the limp rabbit that appeared to be dead. I began to pray.

"Dear God, please don't let my rabbit die. I know you can save him please God."

While I was praying, my sister was massaging the rabbit's chest. I guess you can say she was giving the rabbit CPR. Within seconds, the rabbit started to move and without an explanation, the rabbit opened up his eyes and flopped over on his belly. She laid the rabbit on the floor and it started to hop as if nothing was wrong. We fed it some water and lettuce and it grew and lived like normal. It was a miracle. I know that this sounds unbelievable. However, I know that God had a hand in that experience. It was a divine intervention. My sister was amazed. I was so glad she was there to witness the experience.

Several times in my life, I can remember getting hurt and passing out. When my mother confronted the doctor, he explained that the fear would take my breath from my body. He recommended that my feet be elevated to return the blood to my head. How true is this experience with our relationship with God? We become discouraged, depleted, sometimes angry, and full of rage. Situations are out of our control and we fall into a pit of helplessness. Limp like the rabbit with no way to find our way back to life, as we know it and want it to exist.

Only by the grace of God, can we find our way back to living. He sees us in distress and he stops to pick up our limp soul and lifts our feet to allow the blood to return to our brain so we can again function as a whole person. The blood allows the brain to work properly and gives us the strength needed to continue in life. Just as Jesus died on the cross and shed his blood so we can have life everlasting, I believe he also gives us wake-up calls with divine interventions.

Do you feel helpless? Has the blood of life left your body? Maybe you should connect with someone who truly loves you and will give you the desire to redirect the excitement that is living somewhere within your spirit. Pray for strength and refuel your soul. It never hurts to feed off of the word of God. You will notice throughout this book I refer to verses in the Bible that validate my points. I hope you will take the time to look them up.

Nursing School

Romans 8:28 tells us that God's purpose for people was not an afterthought. His purpose for our lives was decided before the foundation of the world. If this is true, then why has he allowed some people to fail when they clearly feel that they are doing God's will?

I remember asking my mom what she thought I would be when I grow up. Her reply was, "I just want you to make it out of high school."

It was always my feeling that God was calling me into the medical field. I applied to many local schools of nursing. I was accepted and enrolled into a two-year nursing program. I bought my books and took all the Science classes needed before entering my nursing clinical classes. It turned out that after a year in nursing, I learned that I did not take it serious enough to study long hours and work with sick people. The creative side of me kept leaving the room to socialize and forgetting important steps of procedures. Later in life, I learned that I have some ADD characteristics. Forgetting to chart and loosing important papers, became a serious offense.

I also had problems pushing very sick people on the elevator. I would push the button and try, as I may, could not get the gurney to go forward into the elevator. After several tries, I started laughing hysterically and then realized that I was entertaining the nurses at the nurse's station and other students who were also standing nearby. Asking for help, because you are a first time driver, was not humorous either. Thank goodness, my patient was unconscious and was not aware that I was having trouble pushing her onto the elevator. I also remember being punished by my instructor because of my behavior. As my punishment, I was the student chosen to do the first catheterization of a patient. My instructor was testing my skills and asking questions from the homework given the week before.

"One of you will be chosen to catheterize a patient before the week is over," said our instructor.

I have never won a thing in my life, not one drawing or prize at a party. As luck would have it, I won. I was the first student nurse to show the small group how to catheterize a male patient. I was only twenty-one and the patient was a good-looking male of thirty. It was one of the most embarrassing times of my life. I would do my best. But I messed up again and contaminated the sterile field used in the procedure. That afternoon in class, I was an example to show the other students what not to do when working with a sterile field. I wanted to cry. Is this what God has planned for my future? If this is my lifetime career, I was not having fun. The patients loved me and I enjoyed working with the patients. However, I was not focused on the task at hand. My best asset was giving shots.

I had much practice giving shots. One patient requested me to give his pain injections. I could do basic nursing. Giving baths, changing bandages, and giving shots were perfect. Unfortunately, this is not all you are required to do as a nurse. It was clear to me that this was not what I wanted to do the rest of my life.

So why did God make it so clear that this was the direction I should choose for my life? I was accepted into a school of nursing where only 133 students were chosen. Three hundred students applied and I was one of the one hundred and thirty-three students who passed the test and made it into the program. I was sure that it was a God thing.

Later I understood why God put me in the nursing field. It was plain to see his divine intervention. A few years later, my grandfather died and my aunt was in the hospital recovering from a surgery. She asked her doctor if she could attend the funeral out of town. She needed pain shots and a bandage changed twice a day. I was the only one who was able to take care of her. With instructions from the doctor, I gave her shots, changed her catheter, and changed bandages from an open wound.

When other members of the family needed someone to take care of them, I was always there as their nurse. My mother, my mother-in-law, my husband's aunt and our minister. I was always there for others who needed my help in times of crisis. I was the only family member available to help at hospitals and give home care when friends were sick. My nursing also came in handy when I married a doctor. I was able to understand language written in his prescriptions and help him at his office when needed.

Later in life I had my share of hospital procedures. Knowing what was coming next prepared me to endure the pain. I must also mention that I had two active boys and as you know with boys there are always cuts, broken bones and stitches. We had plenty of accidents. Bundling up a crying, bleeding child was not a difficult task when you understand what procedures will follow. I am sure God took that in consideration by allowing me to give birth to boys and to become an elementary school teacher. My limited nursing experience became a blessing in both careers. Thank you, God, for that divine intervention.

Jesus Really Does Save! The Lifeguard

We were lucky to have one of the first in-ground pools in the neighborhood. One of my mother's goals was each of her children should learn to swim. We all took swimming lessons at an early age. After we had the pool built, she decided to hire a swimming teacher from the YMCA to come teach lessons to her childcare children. This was a wonderful idea and a great opportunity for young children back in the seventies. Today it would be impossible to offer swimming lessons at a private home. Can you imagine the risk for lawsuits?

Many children learned to swim in that pool. I wanted to be a certified lifeguard just in case we ever had anyone to fall in by mistake. The pool was eight and a half feet deep. The teacher from the YMCA came at night to certify some friends and I to become lifeguards. When our class was over, all we had to do was go to the YMCA and take the test. The summer came and went and I never made it to the YMCA to take the final test. I thought about it often. What a waste of time and money that summer. I could have worked summers as a lifeguard.

Twenty years later, I went to pick strawberries with my mother and sister at a local country farm. While they were buying homegrown vegetables, I walked over to a lake and watched a couple of boys who were harassing an older woman. She looked like she had dementia and was not willing to go with the boys to the platform dock where a small boat with paddles was located. She kept screaming, "Leave me alone!" Her granddaughter was setting on the side of a hill breast-feeding a little baby. She was also screaming, "Come on guys, and leave my grandmother alone." The two boys kept pulling her onto the dock until they had her in the wobbly boat. Standing up rocking the boat, the two teenage boys laughed as the old woman continued to cry and scream. They pushed the boat out to the middle of the lake and continued to rock the boat back and forth even faster. The girl on the hill was now begging the boys to stop, but they continued until the boat flipped over and all three went under.

I cannot begin to tell you how I felt. I was so angry. I remember hearing the screams of the girl on the hill asking someone to save her grandmother. The two boys bobbed up and grabbed hold of the boat. There was no sign of the grandmother. It seemed that several minutes went by and still no grandmother. Before I could even surmise the situation, I found myself in the water swimming toward the woman. I dove into the middle of the lake and grabbed the woman by the shoulder of her dress. Then I pulled her to my side and crossed my arm in front of her body. I swam to the side of the lake and when I reached the side of the water, I pulled her up on the grass and rolled her over on her side. Water was oozing out of her mouth. When I looked up, I saw an EMS worker running toward us. I moved out of the way and they begin to work on her. At this point I felt a chill come over my body. I could not believe that I saved this woman. Yes, she did live and they rushed her to the hospital. The young girl with the baby thanked me for saving her grandmother and the last time I saw the boys they were screaming for help holding onto the boat. A girl from the other side of the lake jumped in and pulled them to safety. Another EMS arrived and my mother and sister were running toward me. They were under the impression that I was the one that fell into the water.

"What in the world did you do?" questioned my sister.

"Are you all right?" asked my mom.

"I am just fine I just saved that woman there on the ground," I responded.

"No!" said my mom.

"Yes, she did," said a woman and man standing close by the lake.

"We watched her from the restaurant over there on the other side of the lake."

"She jumped in dress and all. It was amazing." The couple complemented.

I was so tired that I could not talk. Then I begin to shake. It never occurred to me that I swam to the middle of the lake until we started home. It was a hot day, July 7, and my sun dress was quick to dry. I took the keys out of my purse and started to drive home. As I started the car, I looked at my sister and said, "I can't drive. My arms and legs are shaking and my heart is beating out of my body."

"When you calm down, we want to hear exactly what happened," said my mom. Shaking my head, I looked out the window and tried to relax. Then I recalled the event and both of them were amazed.

"It was like someone or something jumped into my body," I said.

"I just can't explain it." I continued.

Thinking back, I could see that the life saving lessons were not a waste of time after all. I think God was giving me the skills I needed to save this woman, even if it would be twenty years later. Was this a divine intervention? I think so. Call it what you may, but I would not have jumped into that water if I had stopped to think of all the things that could have happened to me. It was definitely a God thing.

Remembering That God is the Great Physician: Cancer

So often, when we get sick, we listen to doctors and professionals. We forget that we have a built-in doctor that knows our bodies, because he made our bodies. I am not saying we should not listen to these professionals. I am just trying to reinforce the power of prayer. If you are not a believer, what could it hurt? We tend to believe in ghost, mysterious sightings and other things, so why not take a chance with prayer. It could not hurt and you might just find out that it works.

I am over fifty and I am still not sure what God wants me to do in my life. I pray that God will use me to do what he needs me to do for him. I was a teacher by profession. I enjoyed teaching and watching students discover new things. This process does not stop when we leave school. Let your wisdom and strength keep you in the spotlight of life. I think that we are born with the gift of sensitivity to things that are wrong in our bodies. How many stories have you heard where people knew that their bodies were not working just right, but they have trouble convincing the medical world? Why not ask God to help you convince the physician who is trying to diagnose you.

When I was twenty-seven years old, I started to have bladder infections. I went to my family doctor and he gave me some powerful medicine to eliminate the pain in my lower abdomen and back. The medicine worked for a while, but as the medicine wore off, the pain returned. When I returned to my family doctor, he gave me more medicine and said he wanted to see me in three weeks. Again, the pain went away but when the medicine was out of my body, the pain returned. There was never any blood in my urine. This activity continued for five long months. I went to the emergency room one night because I thought someone there just might have the answer. Instead, the doctor gave me the same medication that my family doctor gave me. Again, the pain returned when the medicine ran out of my body.

After several visits to my family doctor, I went to see a urologist. Again, the urologist gave me medicine and said it was just an infection. He told me to give it a few weeks and come back to see him. I was getting worried. I had taken medicine all summer and now it was time for school to start. I had to get some answers before I started back to school. I could not get to the restroom when school started. We only get lunch and one small break. The teacher's restroom was on the first floor across the building. There was only two times to use the restroom. Most of the time you choose to relieve yourself or grab a drink in the lounge. There was never time for both. I could usually hold it until school was over on the days I did not get a break. It is just something that every elementary school teacher learns when she does her student teaching.

My drink of choice was Tab and I would start out with one in the morning, grab one at lunch and one after school. Then again, I would have a Tab for dinner. I needed water with the medicine the doctor was giving me, but the water in the water fountain was rusty tasting and I hated to see even the kids use it. In the seventies, we did not have bottled water, so my Tab was replacing my water.

The urologist saw me two more times. Again, he felt that it was just an infection. I knew better. I just wanted someone to believe me. Then one day I was working at school, and I was in so much pain that I had problems bending over. I was trying to put up a bulletin board, but screamed with pain. When I went downstairs to the bathroom, I saw a small drop of blood. I knew that I should not be in this much pain with a small bladder infection that I had treated for months with strong medicine. I went to the office and asked if I could use the phone. I took the urologist number out of my purse and called his office. He said to come on in the office. He sounded discussed but said he would see me.

I left school and went home. My sister drove me to the doctor's office. When I went back to see the doctor the nurse put me in his office. He was very frank with me.

"Are you sure you had blood in your urine?" he asked.

"Yes, sir," I replied. "I am in so much pain right now. What should I do?" I questioned.

"I have given you every kind of medicine they make for the bladder. It seems that nothing is working on you. I don't think there is blood in your urine or you have any cysts. Only little old woman have cysts in their bladder and you are not a little old woman," he lectured.

"What should I do?" I asked.

"The next step is to put you in the hospital and do a cystoscope of the bladder. You will have to check into the hospital and stay overnight."

"Okay, I'll do it," I responded.

The doctor set the procedure for the next Monday. I had a long weekend taking hot baths and pain medicine. On Monday, I checked into the hospital and spent the night. The next morning the doctor came in. Again he stressed that he felt that this was not necessary, but he promised that he would, "get to the bottom of my problem."

I went into surgery feeling that the doctor was angry with me. When I woke, my family was standing at the side of the bed. My mom and sister told me that I had a tumor removed from my bladder. I didn't understand what they were talking about until the doctor came into the room. He explained that I had a malignant tumor and that he took it out right away.

"You understand I could get in trouble for not waking you and getting your permission. But I didn't want to wake you and upset you just to put you to sleep again for another surgery," he explained.

"I feel one hundred percent sure that I got the entire tumor. The tumor was the size of a dime and it was growing upward toward the bladder. No wonder you were in pain," said the doctor. "I was certainly surprised to see a tumor. You are the youngest patient I have ever seen with a bladder tumor. You understand that it was cancer don't you," asked the doctor.

It didn't really hit me because I had never known anyone with cancer. I didn't know how serious cancer could be. I did not know anything about chemotherapy.

"I am not going to recommend chemotherapy since I scraped the side of the bladder. I'll look into your bladder again in three weeks to see if anything is growing. For right now, I am going to let you go home in a few days and then come back to the hospital for another scope." He stated.

As the doctor left the room, he said, "I am sorry you had to go through all of this. It was a surprise to find that tumor. From now on I am going to listen to my patients."

I smiled at him and he looked back at me and pointed to the roses on the side table.

"The roses are from me. I am sorry I did not believe you. I know you will feel better soon. I'll be back tomorrow to see how you are doing," he said as he left.

I never had chemotherapy and for ten years, I had scopes to check for cancer. Fortunately, I have never had a sign of cancer since that day. The doctor is retired, but from that day on, he was my best friend. God used my case to help my doctor to scope more young women when they complained with bladder pain.

I listened to my body and that small voice that pushed me onward to have more evaluations. Again, God saved my life. He had work for me to do. If I had continued to live with the tumor, the cancer would have taken my life. Was that a God thing? A divine intervention? I call it a miracle and another event to share how God takes control of our lives.

Another Giant Step: Should We Adopt?

I had been married for two years. My husband and I were in our thirties. We had not really talked about when we were going to start our family. I remember sitting by the pool with him and talking about the right time and the right month. Being a teacher, I wanted to have my children in the summer so I wouldn't have to take off from school. We counted the months and decided that October would be the right time so our baby would be born in June. This would give me the summer to get ready to go back to school. I had a doctor's appointment that next week and I asked her about going off the pill so I could start our family. When the doctor examined me, she had a strange look on her face. I knew something was wrong.

"Mrs. K I want you to have an ultrasound of your abdomen. I can feel a tumor inside of your uterus. It is quite big and easy to feel," She said.

"What does all of this mean?" I asked.

"I am not sure, but it feels like it is about the side of a tennis ball."

"I understand, but do we need to have it removed or what?" I asked.

How could this be happening again? I thought. *What if it is cancer? Then what will I do?*

All these questions were running wild in my mind. The doctor told me to make plans to have the test the next day. As I walked to the nurse's station to make the appointment for the ultrasound, I was trying to think of what I was going to tell my husband and family.

I went to my mom's house. We called my sister to come over. We sat there thinking about what the doctor had said. They said I should wait until my husband got home from work to tell him what was going on. I agreed to make him a big supper and talk to him.

That night, my husband decided to take off from work and go with me to the hospital. We had not thought of the possibility that I might have to have a hysterectomy. In our mind, we just figured that the doctor would take out the tumor and everything would be all right. Later that day after I returned from the hospital, my doctor called me and told me that she wanted me to go ahead and get the tumor out. She didn't feel that it was cancer; however, she did not want to take a chance. The nurse set up a date and time for that next week. My husband took off work, and on Monday of the next week we scheduled the surgery.

The night before the surgery, I had all the blood test and was ready for the doctor. My husband and I sat in the room thinking it would all be over soon and everything would be just fine. After supper, the doctor came to visit. She sat with us and started to talk about the ultrasound.

"The tumor was very big. Bigger than I thought it would be," said the doctor.

"I just want to prepare you for the possibility of a hysterectomy. If the tumor has attached itself to the wall of the uterus, then we may have to take out your female organs. How do you feel about the fact that you may never be able to have children?" she questioned.

Rich and I looked very surprised at each other.

"I don't think we have ever talked about that." I replied.

"We had planned to start our family in the next few months," said Rich.

"We definitely want children," he replied.

I could see the look on my husband's face, and he looked like he wanted to cry. It was reality now that the doctor explained that the surgery was for real and most likely going to be a hysterectomy.

"You might want to have some time alone to talk about the possibility of adopting children. Many people adopt children nowadays. Talk about it and if you need me to find someone to come talk to you after the surgery, we can arrange that to happen. Now get some sleep tonight and I will see you early in the morning," said the doctor as she left for the evening.

The next few minutes were silent. We held hands and looked at each other as if we had never met. I could see the hurt in my husband's eyes. He was trying hard not to cry. I took my hand

and touched his face. As tears ran down my face, I mouthed the words "I am sorry."

He looked at me and he tried to speak but the lump in his throat would not allow him to utter a sound. I have never seen my husband so upset and disappointed. At this time, I started crying aloud and could not stop. The loud weeping never made a difference in my husband's posture. He continued to sit there frozen in time. There was so much to say, but neither of us knew how to say what we were thinking. I felt like I was the biggest failure that God had put on this earth.

This could not be happening to us. We were the perfect couple together. After all, I prayed that God would bring me a Christian husband and a happy home. I pictured that happy home with two children playing together in the back yard. Why did God wait so long to bring me that Christian spouse? I am too old to have children. After all most women, have their children in their twenties. Through all my tears, I doubted God and maybe even blamed God.

"Why me, God?" I prayed. "Why do I have to go through this 'life punishing ordeal?'"

"If there is any way you can give us a baby, please give us a miracle," I continued.

I was silently praying that pray over and over. Just as my husband and I started to talk, a nurse opened up the door and announced that she was going to take me to x-ray. My husband followed.

I continued to cry all the way down to the x-ray room. When the x-ray tech looked at me, she asked why I was so upset. I explained that I was going to have a surgery and all about the fact that we may never be able to have children. This medical person was so out of line. She begins to tell me that having children was a hard job.

"Being a mother is not all it seems to be. I have children and they couldn't care less about me. You raise them and give them the best years of your life. When they grow up, they leave home and you never get to see them unless they need something. You and your husband can save your money and travel." She advised. "Now stop crying. You don't need a kid," she continued.

I wish I had her name. That was not what I needed to hear at that moment. Why did she think she could tell me how I should feel? Now I was praying harder. I knew that somehow Rich and I were going to be parents. "God please, hear my prayer. I know you can do miracles. I need a miracle, God," I begged.

I continued to cry all the way back up to my room. Rich was ready to talk now. I saw a disappointment in his face. "I always thought that we would have children," he said.

"How do you feel about that" he asked?

I am around children all day and it will be fine if I just take care of other people's children.

"It's okay with me," I said.

"I have been with children all my life and I am sure I will be working or taking care of children for a long time," I announced.

"It's really okay with me. I promise, Rich."

I didn't realize that he needed me to say it's not what I expected and I too was upset with the possibility that we would always be childless. I thought I had said everything he wanted me to say.

"Well, I want to be a father. I want children of my own and I absolutely do not want to adopt a baby that does not belong to me," he replied.

I was very shocked! "How can you say that honey?" I asked.

"It might be okay with you, but I need to marry someone who wants to have children. I want those children to have my genes and be a part of her and I. That's the way it should be," he said.

My husband had never been as clear as he was at that moment. He wanted children and maybe he didn't want me if I couldn't provide them for him. I started to cry again. He walked over to the window and ignored the hurt that I was feeling in my heart. Could he really leave me, I wondered?

The nurse came into the room and gave me some sleeping medicine to help me sleep well before the surgery. When she left the room, Rich kissed me goodnight and left the room.

I continued to cry until I fell asleep.

Early the next day Rich and all of my family came to my room to say good-bye before the surgery. Our minister was there to say a final prayer. No one mentioned the type of surgery I was going to have. Everyone kissed me as the nurse pushed the gurney down the hall and into a nearby elevator. Soon I was drowsy and the doctor was telling me that it was going to be over very soon. The last thing I remember was scooting over on to the operating table.

Two hours later, I was back in my room. I remember looking for a familiar face.

"Honey, wake up it's all over," said Rich.

He was now rubbing my face with his hand and looking down into my face. The sting of the anesthetic was still hanging on to my body as I tried to open my eyes wide enough to see everyone standing around me in my room.

I remember hearing people laughing. I was dizzy and my stomach gave me pain. I recognized my family and the voice of my husband. He leaned over the bed and said something that I would repeat many times throughout our marriage.

"Honey, wake up. You have a uterus two ovaries, and a husband that is willing." The next thing I saw was our minister backing into the hall laughing uncontrollably. My whole family was laughing and my husband had a smile on his face. Along with the smile, he had a tear rolling down his face. I couldn't figure it all out at first until, he leaned down over me and quietly said, "You didn't have a hysterectomy."

"What happened?" I asked.

"The tumor was on the outside of the uterus instead of the inside. The doctor took the tumor off and left you everything you need to have a baby," said my husband. I realized that this could not be the case. I thought about it for a few minutes and then asked, "How could that be, the doctor felt it when she examined me?"

"I have no idea," said my husband. "It had to be a miracle."

"What did the doctor say?" I continued.

"She is as surprised as we all are," repeated my mom.

"We can start our family now," said Rich. I was sure that my family had misunderstood the operation. I had to talk to the doctor myself. Later on that afternoon, she came into my room. She said that when they cut into my abdomen, this big tumor pushed out. It was as big as a tennis ball, or maybe bigger. She explained that they took another x-ray, confirming that this was the tumor on the ultrasound. She had no explanation why she felt it inside the uterus.

"I can't tell you how I was able to feel the tumor or why it showed up inside of the uterus on the ultrasound. I'll just say it was a miracle," explained the doctor.

In October of 1984, I became pregnant. On June 21st 1985, I had a nine pound six ounce baby boy. He was big and beautiful.

He was the center of our universe. Three years later again in October, I became pregnant with another baby. On June 7, 1988, just two weeks short of a year, I delivered another baby; eight pounds and eleven ounces. Just like the first baby, he was beautiful. I was able to return to teaching in the fall. Both boys went to daycare or grandma's house while I enjoyed teaching. I can't imagine life without them. They will never know how much we love and thank God for giving us these two precious men. They are the heartbeat of our family. I pray for them daily. I ask God to protect them and grow them into wonderful Christian men. Again, I ask, "Is this a coincidence or a divine intervention?"

If you are lucky enough to be blessed with children, don't forget to ask for protection for them from the world. Pray that you have given them knowledge to choose wisely their friends, spouse, and other life choices. Pray for their health and welfare. Pray that they know Christ and are not ashamed to share him with others. It's one of the best gifts you can give them, especially when they are grown and no longer interested in your advice.

Praying For a Miracle

I can't tell you how many times I have prayed for a miracle. Sometimes it happens; other times it has not been in God's will. I do know that God can perform miracles. It happens everyday. Some will make the news; others will never be announced or shared. God arranges the miracles. When we see his work, I think we should share it with as many people as we can. We need to reaffirm the power of God and how he works in our lives.

When our first baby was born, we found out that he had a heart mummer. The doctor didn't seem concerned, so we just believed that it was something he would outgrow. To our surprise, he was sick every month of his life. One day at a doctor's visit I saw a new doctor in the practice. She listened to his heart and suggested that we take him right away to a pediatric heart specialist. Wasting no time, she set us up with a doctor that afternoon. After x-rays and an electrocardiogram we were told that he needed surgery right away. His case was pushed up to the front of the case load listed for the heart board. All the doctors agreed that he be scheduled for surgery at the end of the week. Again, we prayed for a miracle.

I was nine months pregnant and feeling tired. I had already dilated five centimeters. We spent the night at the hospital with him before the surgery. The next morning they took him for surgery to fix the huge bulge in his aorta. He had an enlarged heart and a malfunctioning valve. His surgery was about seven hours long. My husband and I walked the floor waiting for answers. I was sure that I was going to have the baby any minute. Even the nurses were worried.

After several hours the doctor came off the elevator. He told us that our boy was doing fine. The doctor put a patch into him, and the boy would have a lengthy stay in the hospital.

In the next breath, the doctor continued, "His leg was burned during surgery by a cauterizing tool. It was a mistake that shouldn't have happened. It burned to the bone and I did surgery while he was out. He should be fine. It won't affect his leg or ability to walk. There will be a scar, but he should grow out of it."

At first we didn't understand what had just been explained to us. Looking at each other, my husband and I realized that the operation went fine, but the nurse helping the doctor laid the tool on his leg. We first stopped to pray and thank God for sparing his life. Then we prayed for his leg and quick recovery. Our family on the other hand wanted us to press charges. As we walked into the room to see our son, his recovery nurse was standing there waiting for us. She called us by our first name and we recognized her as the wife of one of my husband's colleagues. We had socialized with them several times. She told us that this was a wonderful job. She would be his only nurse for the evening. She promised she would keep us informed with everything that happened in the ICU. The parent hospital rooms were all taken, but this nurse found me a room at the nearby Holiday Inn. My husband spent the night in the waiting room. Two weeks later after my son's last visit to the doctor, I went into labor that night and had my second child. What a divine intervention. A new doctor diagnosing his problem just in time to save his life. A nurse who knew us and spent extra time caring for my son and my delivery, just as we finished with all the doctor visits. How ironic that my baby waited for my two year old to recover so I could fully focus on giving birth.

So why did we not file a law suit against the nurse? Simple, we wanted to extend grace to her just as God had extended to us. I felt that God saved my son, and we were just so grateful that he was going to live a normal life. God gave us a miracle. So I wanted to extend the same to the nurse who was probably crying and praying that she was not going to court for an accident that was careless. I am sure she had already been punished by the doctor and her supervisors. We will never know if she lost her job. But I am sure God knows what really happened.

There was another surgery in 2007.

Just as the doctors had explained at the time of Brad's first surgery, the artery that was repaired began to bulge as his body grew. Once a year since his operation he visits the doctor and is given tests to see how his heart is working. In 2007, the doctor looked at his EKG and his echocardiogram and ordered an MRI.

Looking at the tests the doctor called and told us that we needed to come back to the hospital. Brad had already gone back to school, so we had to call him home. The reports from his tests went before the heart board. It was decided that Brad needed two surgeries.

I could not believe that we were going to go through this again. Brad was not a happy camper. He had just graduated from college and was ready to get his life started. He had applied for jobs in his field of expertise, and had interviews waiting for him.

His first operation was in August. We again camped out in a room while a surgery nurse gave us a minute by minute report of the surgery. After several hours the doctor came out and told us that everything went fine. Brad was in much pain but he was able to leave the hospital in about three days. It was a relief that he was healing and doing so well. I brought him home with us and took care of him until his next surgery. He had not lived at home for four years so he was not excited about spending time at home lying around his old bedroom. Fortunately for us, he has so many friends, that he had people in and out of the house almost everyday. His brother was still home so they had time to be together.

I loved having my son home, but I was still thinking about the second operation now planned for October. The summer came and went so quickly. Soon the day arrived for the second surgery. I prayed a lot in those three months. I knew this was the worse operation of the two. This operation was going to repair the valve of his heart. Again we camped out in that room waiting for the minute to minute update on our son. It was a huge worry and all of a sudden I started to have chest pains. I clutched my chest and took a deep breath. I told my friend sitting next to me. "I feel like I am having a heart attack."

Just as I took a deep breath and leaned against the wall, the nurse came into the room and reported, "The doctor has his heart out and everything went fine."

"The doctor is going to look at his valve to see if it can be repaired or if he'll need a new one. I'll be back when I have more news," she explained.

I could not imagine the doctor holding my son's heart in his hands. The one God so gently placed there to give him life. As his mother, I gasped and started to cry. The ministers and friends in the room all gathered to pray. I know God was in that operating room with my son.

Brad did not have to have a replacement, only a repair. After a few hours he went to ICU, where we spent the night at the hospital with him. I knew that he would have a breathing tube and IVs everywhere. I got to see him. We waited for him to wake-up. About five-o-clock in the morning, Brad was asking for us. He had a breathing tube in and could not speak. The nurse came to get me and walked me back to the ICU. She had promised him that she would take out the tube when his blood pressure went down. She was trying to get him to relax.
As I walked into the room, his eyes were closed. I picked up his hand and held it. Brad immediately opened up his eyes. He knew right away it was my hand. I placed his long fingers and big long hand between my two hands. Then I kissed his forehead. He was trying to say something to me, but the nurse reminded him that he should not speak. She took his blood pressure and it had gone down quite a bit. The nurse then looked at me and said, "It just took a mother's touch."
Brad knew everything was going to be fine. He knew I would answer his questions so that he could find out how things went. I stood there as the nurse took off the respirator for Brad to speak to me.
"You're doing fine, son. It's all over." Just a few weeks after he left the hospital, he got a job and moved to Chicago. A divine intervention! The mother in me cried. I had to once again place him in God's hands.

Always Call Upon the Lord

When my second son was just two years old, we moved into a new house. It was beautiful – just what we had dreamed we would own one day. He was just starting to crawl. I would place him in a walker to encourage him to use his legs in a walking position. It didn't take him long to figure out how to work the walker. He could move across the room so quick that we couldn't keep up with him. We had someone always on call to watch our little torpedo so we could move into our new house.

We choose a ranch-style house so the boy's bedrooms would be on the same level as the master bedroom. The only steps we were worried about were the long steep stairs leading down to the basement. They were carpeted and had rails. I had a baby gate for the top of the steps. Each time the baby would approach the gate, we would warn him that he would fall. Because it made us anxious, he would back away and play in the family room. We thought that we had it under control.

One day when I was home by myself, I put him in his walker and started supper. I was preoccupied with cooking when I saw the walker pass me and head toward the steep stairs. I ran as fast as I could, but it was too late. I watched my child tumble down each stair hitting his head repeatedly on the wall, with his body slipping through the walker. He hit the bottom of the door and knocked his head against the door frame. His neck was bent between the front of the walker and the door hinge. I screamed, then prayed that God would not let my baby die. Please let him be all right. I stood there knowing that when I get to the bottom of the stairs, I would find my baby dead. He did not move or make a sound.

Crying and praying, I made it to the bottom of the steps. When I picked the walker up off of his head, my heart was in my mouth.

"Hi mommy," came out of that precious baby's mouth.

How could this be? He didn't cry. He didn't whine. He wasn't hurt. Nothing was broken and he didn't have one bruise on his face, arms, or legs. I immediately prayed, "Thank you, God." I declared on that day an angel was beside my baby and lifted him to safety. I didn't see anything unusual but I did see my child beaten up with his neck twisted to the side of his head. I also picked up the walker. It could not have saved him but helped to twist his body in that awful shape. I kissed him over and over as I thanked God for the miracle I had just witnessed. I know it was a divine intervention. Again, God had intervened in my life. My sons are the love of my life and God has saved each one of them for a reason. I know this story is hard to believe, but all I can claim is what really happened. I watched as this impossible event controlled the fate of my son.

I believe being in the permissive will of God, allows a person to become spirit filled. Spirit filled allows God to use you as the person who can intervene toward situations that only God controls.

It may be the earnest prayer for your baby's safety. It may be giving money to a stranger in need or praying for someone who you have never met. There have been times when I have been sitting in a hospital waiting room and felt the need to pray for someone who is keeping watch over a loved one in intensive care. I admit that most of my prayers have been silent because I felt out of place approaching strangers. Nevertheless, I prayed. Did God answer my prayers? I really don't know. The need to intervene was certainly in my heart and soul. I feel that this is a form of divine intervention. You might not know what is wrong, but you know that something is not quite right. I do know that he was there to protect my baby because I was able to witness his power.

How many times have you dreamed about a long lost friend, or had thoughts about someone who you haven't seen in years? When you call them or see them, you find out they have some problem or needs. Is this a divine intervention? I believe it is. Especially if you have the means to solve the problem. I believe listening to your spirit is obeying God's will. If God has given you the resources to help a person and you feel convicted to do so, then follow your spirit. Reach out to those in need. Remember this is not a key to heaven. We are not rewarded for things we do for others. It is our responsibility to be a vehicle for God to intervene. I don't believe that God keeps score.

Works will not get you to heaven. Good works will definitely help you to pass on the spirit of kindness that others may pass on to someone else.

The Lump

In 1987, I went to the doctor for my yearly checkup. By this time I had already been through back surgery and had one ovary removed. I was hoping this visit would not reveal that there would be more surgery. During the visit my doctor found more tumors and suggested that we just keep a watch on things for now. Then she sent me for a mammogram. I hate that visit and the whole process. I know it is necessary for me since I have already had cancer, I grin and bare it, literally. This time when the nurse asked me to wait in the room until she had the x-ray read. I agreed and pulled the paper vest as tight around me as possible. It seemed that I was sitting there forever. Soon the x-ray technician entered the room and asked me to come back to the table for one more squeeze. Realizing that I was still trying to hide what was still impossible to hide, I tore the paper vest and gave up the modesty. Now I was sitting in the cold little dressing room holding the rest of the paper in front of me. The x-ray technician knocked on the door and told me to get dressed. When I exited the room she gave me my medical records and a sticky note was attached. The note said that I should call my doctor as soon as possible. This was a first for me.

When I got home, I told my husband what happened. He seemed concerned and insisted that I call first thing in the morning. The next day before I had a chance to call the office, my doctor called me.

"Hi, Mrs. K. How are you today?" she asked.

"Fine, I suppose," I replied.

"I took a look at your mammogram from yesterday and it looks like you have a medium sized lump in your left breast. I am going to send this to a surgeon and they will call you to set up a time for you to come into the office."

"Okay, does it look like cancer?" I asked.

"I don't think so, but we can't tell until we take a biopsy of the lump," she replied.

I agreed to see the surgeon on Monday. That gave me the whole weekend to worry about this visit to the doctor. I immediately gathered my prayer warriors and asked them for prayer.

On Monday the surgeon set me up for a biopsy the next day. Tuesday morning I awoke early and my husband took me to the hospital. When we arrived I was ushered into the mammogram room. The x-ray technician explained that she was going to x-ray me, find the lump, and then place a pin into the lump. This will show the doctor where the lump is located.

I understood the procedure and waited patiently for her to take the picture. Repeatedly she pierced my breast. I was very sore at this point. The x-ray technician seemed worried. She wanted to talk to the doctor. I had no idea what was going on. I asked if my husband could come into the room while she called the doctor. We were both puzzled about the pins sticking in my left breast. She just left them there while she took the x-rays. My husband looked at his watch and asked what time the surgery was scheduled. That is when I realized that we were half an hour past surgery.

Just as we had decided to track down the technician, the door opened and the doctor and technician came into the room.

"Mrs. K, I want to see if I can find the lump. Can you hold still for just one more minute?"

"I suppose so," I replied. Still standing there with four or fine pins hanging out of my left breast.

The doctor was again poking me with pins and trying to find the lump in my breast. Each time he poked me, I was jumping with pain. I realized that he was poking some of the same places that the x-ray technician had already injected with her pins. Then he took an x-ray with the pins. When the x-ray was developed, he took the x-ray from the first exam and compared it with the new one. Holding up both pictures for all of us to see, he shook his head and made the following statement.

"Okay, here is the deal. The lump is gone." We all looked at each other and the doctor showed us where the lump was in the breast.

"You can plainly see the large lump in the breast on this film. We even took it twice the day you were here and you can see it again in this picture." He explained.

"Here are the two pictures taken today. There is clearly no sign of a lump." We both looked at the x-rays and noticed that they were the same pictures and the breast was the same size. He was right; there were two pictures with lumps and two without lumps. The doctor shook his head.

"Dr. K and Mrs. K, the only thing I can say is it's a miracle. I am not going to do surgery unless I can clearly see a lump. Make an appointment in a month and have another test. If everything is all right, we will just keep a watch on your breast."

The doctor shook hands with my husband and then told me to go home and apply ice on my breast. A month later I went back for another exam. There was no lump. Every year since that day, I have had my annual mammogram and to my amazement nothing has ever showed up.

Was this a divine intervention? Wow I was pleasingly surprised. Again God answered prayer.

I talk a lot about prayer. When we pray, we are asking God to protect us by taking us under his wings. When we agree with one another and ask God for protection we must also expect that our prayers are going to be answered. I believe that our prayers do not fall to the ground unnoticed. If God knows each hair on our heads, then he must know what is inside our head. Right? What we think and what we believe.

Even if you are not a believer, you must admit that you have somehow experienced an amazing account of events that just cannot be explained. We all have seen or heard things that were not possible in the realm of this world. So how did it happen? Is it a spirit from beyond? Is it a protector from another entity, or from another life you once lived? Some would like to believe this. It would definitely make a more interesting story. Something that we could explain. If we could stretch our minds that far, then why not just believe what we read in the Bible. If the Bible is only for true believers, then why is it one of the most read books throughout the world?

Personally I truly believe that God has a hand in everything. Even when life is falling apart. Different daily circumstances help us to see the true evidence that God is in control. Day to day miracles continue to exercise the mind helping us to believe that God works best when we are troubled. More often he provides a way to solve the unpredictable problems of dismay.

Even if we are not believers and have never prayed to ask for his help.

Is This Really Necessary?

I suppose I am boring the reader with medical procedures that has surprisingly be preformed on one living soul. I often tell friends not to count on me to be a donor if they are in need of body parts. Everything I have inside my body has been taken out or rewired.

As I mentioned in a previous chapter, I did have bladder cancer at the age of twenty-seven. Problems with bladder infections have since been frequent. After a routine MRI my doctor called me one night around seven-thirty at night. I was totally surprised.

"Lynn, this is Dr. Pail. I am glad I caught you at home. I have had a chance to look over your MRI and I think I see a spot on your liver and your bladder. I really would like for you to go into the hospital and have a biopsy of your liver. After that I will do a cystoscope and see if there is anything in the bladder."

"What are you thinking Dr. Pail?" I questioned.

"I am not sure. I just want to make sure that everything is okay. My nurse will call you tomorrow and set everything up for the biopsy. Talk to you later."

With that he hung up the phone and I sat there on the couch wondering what would happen next. I walked into the living room and told my husband what he had said. Then I called my mother and sister. The last thing to do was pray. After the boys were in bed and my husband was well on his way to sleep, I started to talk to the Lord.

"Well, Lord, here we are again. It's out of my hands and you are in control. Whatever happens I want to know right away what I should do."

My children were still young and the only thing I was worried about was their life. I didn't want them to be raised without their mother. I personally did not want another woman being a mother to my boys. Thinking about that really ticked me off. No! I was determined to be there when they graduate from high school and when they get married. No God! I pray that everything is gong to be just fine. Now more than ever I was praying for a miracle.

The next day, the hospital called and set up everything for me. I had to be there early to go into the hospital for what they call special procedures. It was about six in the morning and my whole family showed up. Before the surgeon placed me into my ever-ready dressing room, he gathered the whole group in a special meeting room with a large table. Richard was sitting by me holding my hand.

Looking around the room at about eight people, the surgeon continued, "Is this everyone?"

We shook our heads as if we were mentally taking role.

"Yes, I think so," replied my husband.

"I just want to explain what we are going to do," said the surgeon.

"This is a special procedure where we go into the abdomen and take a small piece of the liver. There seems to be a large spot on the liver. If we are lucky, we will be able to pierce the liver and not hit the lung or spleen. This is a very tricky procedure. We try not to do them unless we have to. We can see the spot and we will always have it on the x-ray screen. Now, does anyone have any questions?"

I can't remember if anyone asked anything, but I wanted to know if I would be able to feel any pain. The doctor gave me a smug smile and put his hand on my shoulder.

"Mrs. K, I am not going to lie to you, it is a very painful procedure. I will do everything I possibly can to make it easy on you. We can give you a local anesthetic, but it will still hurt as we push it in. We will be very careful to do it quickly and hopefully we will only have to do it once."

There was nothing I could do but agree to do what the doctor suggested. I went into the dressing room and put on my blue and white gown with no panties or bra. Then I waited for the nurse to come in and cover me with a sheet, take my temperature and blood pressure. The nurse started an IV just in case there would be surgery. Then I was pushed into the operating room and waited on the doctor to arrive.

"Here is a cute little hat for your head and booties for your feet," announced a nurse.

"I guess the outfit is complete and I look beautiful," I replied.

I was joking on the outside, but I can tell you I was totally scared to death. If they find cancer they will put me to sleep and take it right there. If so how much has it spread? How long will I live? Will I have to take treatments? Why didn't I ask all these questions before they had me dressed for surgery?

Soon the doctor came in and he pulled up my gown and covered the parts that were not going to be important during surgery. Then using the x-ray machine the liver was located and the abdomen was dabbed with local anesthetic.

"Lynn, try not to move. I will hold your hand and you can squeeze it as hard as you want," informed the nurse. At this point the doctor took a huge, long needle and pushed it directly into my side.

I was not prepared for the total amount of pain that came over my body. I wanted to sit up and scream to the top of my lungs. The pain was the worse than I had ever endured. Again I will compare it to delivering my nine pound six ounce baby boy naturally. The doctor was delighted that the needle was successfully in the center of the liver where the x-ray showed the suspicious spot.

"Take a deep breath Mrs. K and I will be pulling out the needle," said the doctor.

As the doctor pulled out the needle I squeezed the nurse's hand so hard that I think I could have broke the wedding band on her finger.

"It's okay, Lynn" replied the nurse next to my side. "The doctor will give it to the nurse and she will rush it downstairs to the laboratory. It's all over now, but we need you to lay here until we find out the results."

It seemed like hours before the doctor returned to the operating room. Looking me in the face he smiled again and said, "Think you can do that again?"

At first I thought he was kidding me. "Are you serious?" I asked.

"Yes, Mrs. K we need another biopsy just to be sure. I promise to be quick," the doctor encouraged.

The doctor did not say if it was positive or negative. He took his place on the side of my body again and pushed a new needle back into my liver.

I screamed and at this point grabbed both hands of the nurse standing next to me. She held my hands and told me to scream as loud as I wished. The pressure of the pushing was more than I could bear. I was sick to my stomach. I started to black out. Another nurse grabbed a wet cloth and put it on my head. Soon the sample was being rushed back to the laboratory and again I laid there waiting to hear the results.

The doctor came into the room and asked me if I had been on birth control pills. I admitted that I had. Then he said that sometimes these can cause liver problems.

"We want to be positive about this so just relax and rest awhile," he replied.

That was easy for him to say. I was the one lying on the gurney in pain. Why is it doctors always say relax when you are trying to recover from some awful procedure? Do they really know what it feels like to surrender your body and control to someone who you just met a few weeks ago? Does he really care?

It didn't matter whether he did or did not care, you are his patient and he is the only one who can help you. Right?

No, I don't believe he is the only one that can help. I believe God is the only one who can help. When you are lying on that cold gurney in your thin gown, no underwear, a paper hat and paper shoes, it doesn't really matter if your Gucci purse is locked up safely, or your designer shoes and clothes are packed away properly in a closet near by. Nothing matters now except your relationship with a higher being. In my case it was my relationship with God.

Within a few minutes the doctor returned and gave me that half cocked smile. I couldn't tell if he was happy or just trying to convince me that I could grin and bare it one more time. Then he asked the nurse to get my husband.

"Dr. and Mrs. K. everything looks wonderful. There is no sign of a spot on the liver. That is why we took the second biopsy. We wanted to make sure there is nothing to be worried about. I really don't understand why there seems to be a spot on your x-ray. I only know that we saw a spot, but sometimes we just don't understand what happens with the body. Your lab work looks good and shows no signs of a fatty liver. We will do some lab work in a few months and if everything comes out all right then we will assume that there is nothing to worry about."

"Can I go home now?" I asked.

"Yes, you can go home and be thankful you didn't have to have surgery. I'll send a nurse in to help you get dressed. You did just fine Mrs. K. I know it hurts, but I am glad you have good news."

"Thank you, doctor," was all I could say.

When I dropped my gown and put on my clothes, I was thanking God for my miracle. Now I had to have a cystoscope. I started praying right there that it would be something easy and my life would be spared again.

A week later I went to the urologist to get my routine scope that I had been accustomed to enduring for several years. My doctor was glad to see me and teased me as usual about growing up to be an old woman. I was now in my forties. He had been treating me since my late twenties.

The nurse came into the room and the doctor took an extra long look into the bladder. I laid on the gurney waiting for him to give me some hope. I had already prayed and had several people praying for me. This time I was almost sure that everything was going to be fine. As the doctor withdrew the scope, he rolled his chair over to me and smiled.

"There is nothing in your bladder."

"Then why am I here?" I replied.

"Well," explained the doctor, "sometimes the uterus can cast a shadow on the bladder and it will reflect on the bladder and sometimes the liver," he explained.

"I want to see you in six weeks for another scope. If you have any problems just let us know and we will set up a scope earlier." I walked out of the doctor's office with a big smile on my face. I did not have surgery.

Again, was this a divine intervention or just a coincidence?

God Has a Plan for His People

I realize that sometimes the only way God can show us his plan is by sending his angels as messengers. God does not want us to worship angels. He wants us to be aware of angels, as he unfolds his great and mighty plan. They are spiritual beings that are created by God under his authority.

> Hebrews 1:14 (NIV)
> *Are not all angels ministering spirits sent to serve those who will inherit salvation.*

I feel that we are used by God's spirit to influence the will of humans. It may be a friend who feels the urgency to change your path because of a passage read in the newspaper, or a story told on the radio. Perhaps you have been one of God's messengers. You are determined to pass along this information, because you have that nagging spirit that won't let you pass up an opportunity directed by the Holy Spirit. Whatever your role might be in changing the events of the situation, you are used as a messenger. A spirit that is serving others to do good for the glory of the Lord. I am not saying that we are God's angels. We are not angels. However, I believe he uses his angels to guide our spirits. Our inner soul that lives within our bodies.

I remember on 9-11 how many people were spared the tragic event because of a sick child, a car that wouldn't start, stopping to get stamps at the post office, or missing a train or plane. Why did this event take the lives of thousands, yet some were spared because of the misfortune of a morning routine? No one really has the correct answer. Did God have a plan for that person? Is God using him or her to work according to God's will? I wonder if we were to look at the lives of these people today, would we see a divine intervention? How are they making a difference in the lives of others? It is my opinion that God puts people in our lives to make a difference or teach a lesson. Learning never stops. So we should always be aware of those who come into our inter circle that we can learn from or physically help. You may be one of God's messengers and afraid to step forward to follow God's plan for you.

>Psalm 91:11 (New Living Translation)
>*For he orders his angels to protect you wherever you go.*

He was Here!

It was 1991 and my mother-in-law had been admitted again into the hospital for lung problems. I stopped and picked up her eighty year old sister Rosalie, who was eager to see her and find out what the lung doctor was diagnosing. Quietly we entered the room and watched as she rested with the help of medication. Within minutes, the doctor knocked on the door and came into the room. Looking at her chart, he began to explain that the diagnosis looked grim.

"We are giving you all the medication we can to help you breathe. I suggest that you continue to take the medication and keep the oxygen on for twenty-four hours. We can arrange for the oxygen to be delivered to your house," he continued.

Then he patted her on the arm and told her to get some rest.

"If you are better in the morning we will send you home with your new medication and your oxygen." He motioned for us to join him in the hall and we followed him to the nurses' station.

"Mrs. K is not doing well. I really don't see any change in her breathing. I will be back later and see how this new medication is affecting her. There is nothing else we can do here, we might as well send her home to rest and take her treatments. If she responds with this new treatment, then we will let her go home. If she is still having a hard time breathing, we will keep her a few more days," he explained.

Rosalie started to cry. I wouldn't let her go back into the room being so upset.

"You stay here and if she is sleeping, we will go downstairs and get a bite to eat," I explained.

Rosalie agreed to go and get lunch. Since all was quite in the room, I walked back down the hall and took Rosalie by the arm and led her to the elevator. When we got off of the elevator, I could see that Rosalie was too upset to sit at the lunch counter. She put her head down on the table and started to cry.

"I don't know what I will do without her," she explained.

"I can't believe that she has gone down so much," she continued.

"Do you think she will be all right?" she was crying and wiping her eyes.

"Now come on, Rosalie, you can't do this. We need to have faith that the doctor will send her home soon," I encouraged.

"Would you like to walk into the chapel and pray for your sister?" I asked.

"Oh, let's do," Replied Rosalie.

"When we finish eating we will go over and say a little prayer for her. That's all we can do for now," I explained.

The chapel was across the hall from the lunch counter where there were several people eating lunch and looking out into the hall. I opened the big stained glass door and ushered her into the small chapel. By now we were both crying and hugging each other. We walked into the room, which was very dimly lit. The sun was shining through the window and we could see that the room was totally empty. Finding a pew that was close to the altar, we sat down and I begin to pray. When we looked up, a tall African American man was standing next to the pew.

The man looked at us and asked, "Who are you praying for?"

"My mother-in-law and her sister," I replied. "my mother-in-law has emphysema and finds it hard to breath. The doctor is giving her cortisone and breathing treatments every few hours. The cortisone is making her skin thin and her face swell," I reported.

"It's just so hard to see her that way," cried Rosalie. Again I drew Rosalie to my body and put my arm around her as she cried on my shoulder.

"I am a Methodist minister and I just wonder if I could pray for her?" he asked.

"Sure," said Rosalie.

The man said a small prayer as we bowed our head and held each others hand. When he finished we looked up.

"She is going to be all right. She will be going home soon," he replied.

We thanked him slightly but turned to hug each other. When we looked back at the man, he was gone. It had only been a split second. How could he have gotten to the back of the chapel and out the door without us seeing him move? It would have been physically impossible for him to walk out of the chapel and disappear so quickly. I ran to the door and looked out into the hall way. There was no one in the hall. I looked out toward the elevator and no one was standing there. Then I decided to go into the cafe and asked a person sitting at the counter facing the chapel if he saw anyone come out of the chapel.

"No, I saw you and another woman go into the chapel, but no one came out before you," he replied.

"Are you sure?" I asked.

"Yes," he said.

"Thank you," I replied.

I watched Rosalie push through the chapel door. She looked at me and asked about the minister. I explained that he was gone.

"Gone?" she questioned.

"How did he get away so quickly? Where did he come from," asked Rosalie.

"I don't know, but I do know we had a tall big African American Methodist minister in there praying with us. He was so sweet and promised that Dolores would be just fine," I commented.

I then walked into the gift shop and talked with the girl who worked there. I described the gentleman and asked her if she saw anyone who looked like that go by the shop. She was sure that no one had passed the shop. I then questioned her concerning the minister. I asked if she knew of any minister that frequently visited sick patients or went into the chapel next door to pray for patients. The young woman said there were several ministers that frequent the hospital but she did not recall ever meeting a tall African American minister.

Rosalie and I went back up to Dolores's room and she was sitting up in bed and her husband was combing her hair.

"Look what I did," said Jim.

I looked at Rosalie and we both were in shock. How could she be sitting up when she couldn't even lift her head? This was a miracle. We walked out into the hall and discussed what had just happened. We both agreed that we prayed with a minister and we both agreed that she was very ill when we left for lunch.

Later that day the doctor came by the hospital room and felt she had made a remarkable improvement. He released her to go home the next day.

DIVINE INTERVENTIONS 57

I know our prayers were answered that day. Dolores was feeling better that fall. January of the next year, she was back in the hospital and we knew for sure that this was the end.

I know that God had a plan to keep Dolores alive long enough to convince Rosalie that we would be best friends and I would do my best to take care of her. I can see that those long months gave us the time we needed to bond. We went grocery shopping and Christmas shopping. We spent long days at the hospital before she pasted away and when her sister's time was up, she trusted in me. We visited often and I comforted her when she needed someone to talk with.

This divine intervention was not just through prayer. I feel that God sent us an angel. A messenger to give us peace and encouragement. How could this be? I don't really know and can't explain it but it was definitely divine. I do know that there is a spiritual cause to everything that happens in this life.

I was recently telling this story to a cousin of mine. I asked if he believed that God sends angels to help us in times of need? Confidently he began telling me a story concerning something he had experienced.

"When I visited Paris, my friend and I missed the tour bus. We were so lost in that big city. There seemed to be a language barrier that conveniently took place when Americans tried to ask questions. Yes, I knew French, but using it as an American, was not what the French people wanted to hear. Giggling in their native tongue was their way of making fun of a foreign visitor. They were not willing to help us find the train station or give directions to the town where we were staying. Luckily, we found the railway by ourselves and got on the last ride toward what we thought was our destination. Standing in the middle of the transit car, my friend and I started talking about our hotel. A woman standing behind us spoke English and interrupted our conversation. She explained that our hotel was not in the city we had mentioned and that we were going the wrong way. She had a map and showed us the correct directions and told us to get off of the train and take the #2 line to the next city. That will put you right at your hotel. Then she told us to keep the map. Wishing us good luck, we turned to say thanks and she was gone. It was late at night and not many on the train. There is no way she could have vanished like that. The train had not stopped and we walked to the front and back of the car to see if she was sitting on a bench. I looked at my friend and said, No one will believe this!"

I asked, "Was she correct about the hotel?"

"She was right on, and the map she gave us was just what we needed to make it all around Paris," said my cousin. "She left as quickly as she appeared. She was our angel."

There it was – another story about one of God's divine protectors or angels.

The English word Angel comes from the Greek word Ageless. This word means messenger. They are also called Sons of God, Hosts, Allies, and Protectors. There are many ways God speaks of Angels in the Bible. How can we read his word and not totally believe that Angels exist? If God says that he will live in us and protect us then it is only natural that there be some supernatural being that works with him behind the scenes.

I remember when I was a little girl in the second grade. We had a music teacher named Miss Flat. I know this sounds like I am making up her name, but her real name was Miss Flat. She would come to the classroom and teach us songs. She was young, pretty and I wanted to be just like her. I was taking piano lessons, and I loved music so I remember thinking that someday I could be a music teacher just like Miss Flat.

One day she came into our class and before she started teaching us a new song, she asked the class a question. "Who has seen the wind?" Before anyone had a chance to answer my hand went up. I was eager to get her attention and show her I was smart. Instead, I was the only one with my hand in the air. Immediately she acknowledged me and asked me what the wind looked like. Looking around the room I could see that I had said something wrong and just shook my head. I was totally embarrassed. Then she continued to tell me that we can't see the wind, we can feel it, and see it at work, but it is invisible. It made such an impression upon me that I used that poem or song with all of my young students in kindergarten:

"Who has seen the Wind? Neither you nor I, but when the trees bow down their heads, the wind is passing by."

We may not see the divine spirit that rules over us and protects us. When something happens that we can't explain, we realize that we are never alone. God is there and he has his army of angels with him protecting us against harmful situations that we cannot control.

2 Corinthians 4:16-18

Therefore we do not lose heart. Even though our outward man is perishing, yet the inward man is being renewed day by day. For our light affliction, which is but for a moment, is working for us a far more exceeding and eternal weight of glory, while we do not look at the things which are seen, but at the things that are not seen. For the things that are seen are temporary, but the things which are not seen are eternal.

Throughout my life I have felt the presents of angelic assistance. It's a mystery that I can't understand or show to anyone, but I can feel it and I know that there is a special guidance that directs me or inspires me to act upon a situation. I suppose what I am trying to say, is that God has used me many times as one of His messengers.

Walking out of a store one day I saw a young girl asking people for money. I glanced in her direction and didn't really want to get involved until I saw a woman give her a dollar. Then I heard her say, "Thank you but this will not buy enough milk for my baby."

When I heard the word baby my ears perked up. Then I started to watch as she approached others in the parking lot. Pushing my basket back into the store, I listened to her story as I passed her pleading with the next person near by.

"I went to the Kroger grocery store and they kicked me out. They said I couldn't ask people for money in their parking lot. I am desperate and I have to feed my baby," Related the young girl.

I continued to walk back to my car pretending that I didn't see her as I passed her on the sidewalk. Just as I opened the door of my car, I saw her out of the corner of my eye. Oh wonderful! I thought, I am her next victim.

"Miss, do you happen to have any money you could spare me," she continued as I got into my car and shut the door. I rolled down the window and I explained that I had no cash in my purse.

"Thank you," she said, as she started to cry.

Before I could roll up my window a car pulled up beside me and asked if the young girl had asked me for money. It was the woman the young girl was talking to on the sidewalk.

"Yes, she asked me for money," I explained.

"I wish I could have helped her," said the woman.

"She sounded like she was telling me the truth. I just didn't have any cash," said the woman.

"I know," I replied. "So do you think she has a baby or does she just need money?" I asked the woman.

"No! She was across the street asking for money and they ran her off. I am sure she went there because she needed food. She said her baby is young and hungry. Just look at her over there sitting on the curb just crying her little heart out," continued the woman.

"There isn't anything I can do. I gave her all the change I had on me." The woman rolled up her window and drove away. Now I was beginning to think God was speaking to me. What if this girl just wants money for drugs, or beer? What if she doesn't even have a baby?

As I started up my car I drove past the young girl and watched her give up her quest to get money. She just sat there crying. Then I started to pray.

"Dear God if I am to help this girl out please show me what to do."

Quickly I thought about a gift certificate from the Kroger grocery store. If she needs milk, then she could take the gift certificate and get the milk. Everyone there had heard her ask for money for milk, and if she buys anything other than baby formula someone will call her on it.

I drove straight across the street and got stopped by a line of traffic.

"Well, I prayed, if this is my mission God, than let me find a parking spot right in front of the store where I can run in, get the gift certificate, and then run back out."

It just didn't look like that was going to happen. I pulled into the busy parking lot of the grocery. It didn't look as if I would be able to find a parking spot in front. Just as I started my get a way, a car pulled out right in front of me and let the first parking spot open so I could pull in. Ops! God was speaking to me. It was very plain. The line of traffic was gone and I ran without stopping up to the office an asked for a twenty dollar gift certificate. Then I drove back over to the girl and rolled down my window.

"Do you believe in angels?" I asked her.

"What?" she questioned.

"Where is your baby?" I asked.

"At my house with my mom."

"Where do you live?" I continued to ask.

The girl pointed behind the dollar store where she was sitting. She was looking strangely at me wondering how I knew she had a baby. Remember, she didn't tell me she had a baby. Just asked for money.

"Today I hope you believe in God and I want you to know that He has sent me as one of his angels to give you this gift certificate," I explained to the young girl.

I continued to ask her questions.

"Do you have a boy or a girl?"

"A little boy," she smiled.

"How old is he?" I asked.

"He will be eight months old next week."

"Will you promise me that you will tell him something?" I continued.

"Okay," she said as she wiped the tears from her eyes and came closer to the car to retrieve the gift I held in my hand.

"When he is old enough to understand, tell him about your angel and how God provided you with money to buy him milk."

The young girl was now looking at me as if I were an angel. "Okay!" she said.

"You must also promise to take him to church to learn about Jesus and make sure that he learns that God is real and He loves him. I don't ever want you to forget about this money and how you were able to buy milk for your baby. This is important stuff and you need to give God the praise. I am not just an old woman in a green blouse that gives out gift certificates for free. This is a God thing and he wants you to go to church, learn about Him and share God with your baby."

"Thank You," she cried. "I'll do my best. This means a lot."

"Remember you made a promise to me. Don't break it," I said.

I watched as she ran across the street and walked into the store with her money. I was tempted to follow her to make sure she was doing as she said. Then I remembered, I am not God and I should not judge her. My heart was right and I did what I felt God wanted me to do. My job was done.

It Worries Me to Death: Why Worry?

Just when we think that there is no way out of a situation, doors open and needs are met. I have always heard that prayers are answered in God's own time. He can say either yes, no or later. Doesn't this sound like a parent when a child is begging for a favor or a toy?

Prayer is asking our Heavenly Father to give us answers about problems that occur here in this world. Things that we think we cannot control. Most of the time we have no control over the timing of events in our lives. I could write many stories about events that have been totally out of my control. Yet, as time allowed, the problems were taken away from me and fixed by a divine intervention. In every case the key to solving worrisome problems have been earnest prayer. I think sometimes we pray and we are not earnest. Other times we are desperate and we truly believe that God *will* answer prayer.

So does believing in God or a higher power bring a divine intervention? Can you have a divine intervention without a belief in God?

I personally think that each of us can and have experienced an intervention of some kind. In my situations I feel that it was an answer to prayer. I have a strong belief in God. I ask him for help when I need answers. I don't know how I would exist without his assurance that he loves me and wants the best for me. I know this is true because of the promises he gives me in the Bible. If you do not believe that God is the person that brings good into your life and solves your problems, then why not step out on faith and read the following verse in the Bible.

DIVINE INTERVENTIONS

Psalms 27:1
The Lord is the light and my salvation, whom shall I fear? The Lord is the strong hold of my life to whom shall I be afraid?

This verse offers help for today and the future. If you read the whole Psalm you can see that even when the problem attacks us and evil men advance against us, God will give us the strength to be confident that he is in control of the situation.

When I open up my spirit to God, I only need to look at the tremendous power he shows in nature. Someone had to make the Great Lakes and oceans. Someone had to design the huge mountains, the glorious plants that take on a special design in different seasons. Someone had to place the sun and the moon in the sky.

I have to believe that man could not be responsible for all these grand designs. If so we would not need a divine intervention. We could solve our own problems without anyone's help.

Psalm 27:5
For in the day of trouble he will keep me safe in his dwelling; He will hide me in the shelter of his tabernacle and set me high upon a rock.

Psalm 27:13-14
I am still confident of this: I will see the goodness of the Lord in the land of the living. Wait for the Lord; be strong and take heart and wait for the Lord.

I must confess that there have been times that I did not have the strength to wait upon the Lord. When I developed pancreatitis, I was in my forties and had a husband and two young boys at home. I went into the hospital for a simple test to see if the removal of my gallbladder had left behind any gall stones. This procedure was going to be simple and done as an outpatient at the hospital. I had no worries and was sure I would be back home before the boys got home from school.

During the test, I woke up unexpectedly. The doctor was pushing a long tube with a small camera down my throat into my stomach. I was in so much pain and I could not speak. I started to thrash around and the anesthesiologist alerted the doctor. He administered more anesthetic and put me back to sleep. The test was taking longer than expected. The doctor found that an infection had developed in the duct of the gallbladder and was now located in my abdomen. This was going to be more than a simple test. He called my sister over and told her that I had a diseased pancreas. My illness was serious and he admitted me to the hospital. I have never been so sick. I was not allowed to eat or drink for a month. I laid with tubes down my throat pumping green infection out of my body. I was given a blood transfusion. I was not responding to antibiotics. My family was very worried.

Years before my operation, I had become close friends with a nurse. We met in a class held at the hospital where she worked. We would talk on the phone and meet for lunch. We became very close. We shared information about our families and friends.

When I became ill, Lucy called my husband and asked what the family planned to do about my illness. Everyone was puzzled and scared. He explained that the antibiotics were not working and the doctors were doing the best that they could. This was not good enough for my nurse friend Lucy. She suggested that my husband have my doctors call in a specialist. She worked with a doctor who would try different medicines until he could find the right combination of antibiotics to clear infections. Lucy talked to my husband daily. She convinced him that this was the only way I was going to get well. She strongly suggested my husband be part of the physicians' team. Right away my husband talked with my doctors. With nothing to loose, they agreed to call in the specialist.

The next day, I was on several different kinds of antibiotics. I had intravenous lines in both arms and a central line in my chest. Each day there were new treatments. Slowly I began to respond to the medicine. It took a month and several days, but I pulled through the illness.

I believe that my nurse friend was introduced into my life for a reason. Without her connection with my family and the introduction of the new doctor, I am not sure I would have recovered. My husband would not have known to call in a specialist to change the antibiotics. The change was remarkable. Was this a coincidence or a divine intervention?

My gastroenterologist was surprised and so glad that I had beaten the odds. He even wrote off my hospital stay. I still see him when I need him and silently we remember the hard times. I thank God for his knowledge.

I believe that God had a purpose for saving my life. All the prayers that were going out for me were getting God's attention and he had a plan already in place. I have asked my husband many times if he thought that I was going to die.

He always says, "No, I believed that God was listening to our prayers. I had faith."

I am not so sure I was trusting God. I was so sick that I didn't care if I lived or died. It would have been easier for me to give up. That was not in God's plan. You see, he knew that someone would eventually figure out the answer. He gave his plan to my friend Lucy. She passed it on to my family and the team of doctors who were working on my illness. I give thanks to God for this intervention.

I have no idea why God has been such a strong guidance in my life. Why would he listen to me and answer my prayers? Why would he save my life so many times? I am no one special. I was not born of royalty, I have never been famous, and I have no special powers. Why choose me God? Have you ever asked yourself this question?

I learned at a very young age that prayer changes things. As a little girl my grandfather would visit our house. Before we departed to our respective beds, he would gather all the family in his bedroom. We would then kneel at his bedside. My grandfather would pray for each family and each family member. It would seem like hours before we were released to go to bed. If my grandfather thought it was that important, then there must be something to this praying thing.

Growing up in a church atmosphere, I have attended worship services where ministers asked for prayers for sick people. I have seen healing in broken spirits, bodies, and families. I don't suppose I ever asked why these things happened. I always just believed that it was prayer. When we read the Bible, you see that there is a connection between prayer and the power of Jesus. The Bible shows us that prayer changes things. Like a knee jerk reaction, I immediately pray when I have no control over the situation facing me or my family. Does God always answer my prayers the way I ask him too?

"No!" Sometimes he answers me after I have toiled with all kinds of situations. Sometimes he shows me that I need to learn a lesson first. Sometimes it takes years to learn that God was in this situation the whole time. He needed more time to convince me that what I want is not in his will. Whatever happens, I must learn to understand that he is in control and with time the problem will be solved according to his plan.

If you look at all the miracles that have been discussed in this book, you can see that I personally believe that none of them happened by chance. You may ask, "Can something happen by chance?"

First we must look at the word chance. It is just a word, it is not a thing. It is a word that explains or describes mathematical possibilities. Chance has no power. You always know that it will produce one or two difference reactions. There is no way to change the reaction that chance will produce. When you play a game of ring toss, you already know the two different outcomes to expect. It will either fall on the ground or be tossed over the peg. If chance was involved then why did the unexpected happen? Healing of a tumor in the breast is not something that was expected. Therefore I cannot believe that it was chance that changed the situation.

I am not saying that we as born sinners do not take chances. We are human and chance is a human characteristic. We take chances everyday of our lives. I admit we may or may not know the circumstances. If we want something bad enough, we do take chances hoping that we get the response we are looking to gain. We might drive our car on empty taking a chance that we can make it to a gas station. We might cross the street against the light, taking a chance that we don't get hit by a car. In each incident we still know that one or two things are going to happen. We are expecting a good or bad outcome. With interventions, we are not expecting a certain outcome. It surprises us and wow what a difference it can make in our lives.

I Know this is a God Thing: Choosing the Right School

When my son was old enough to go to school, we all were praying that he would be ready, and that he would get into Traditional School. In the 1980s and '90s this was the elite way to educate your child, both developmentally and cognitively. The traditional schools were expecting children to excel at a greater rate than the normal school. Traditional schools also had more to offer as far as socializing your child with others, who were at his or her level. The parents signed an agreement that they would be involved with every aspect of the child's education. There was homework every night and conferences once a month. Unaccepted work was signed and returned to the teacher. Reading was assigned nightly with parents signing an affidavit that the child read for thirty minutes or more every night. Homework was checked off and signed nightly and projects were assigned to be turned in every six weeks.

Feeling that we were the fortunate family having a child in the Traditional School, we would do just about anything to keep up the education that would send our child to Harvard. I say this tongue in check, because I feel like my husband and I were the pupils and we were earning the grades. I dreaded going home after work. My son had so much homework that he would often fall asleep and wake early to finish before school. We did everything we could to keep him interested in school. To our amazement, he learned to like school and was a very good student. He made it all twelve years in Traditional School. We were so proud when he graduated and was accepted into college. Little did I know that Traditional School was not all that strict about behaviors and attitudes. He was learning another kind of education behind our back. How to swear, cheat, and at times when necessary, lie. It would be years later that he would confess this to us.

When our second son started school, we were not as fortunate to get him into Traditional School. The system had changed and went to a form of lottery according to sex and race. Being a white boy was not an advantage. There were many boys born in 1988 and so this dropped his chances of going to Traditional School. He was now going to attend public school and be inter-graded with handicap children and others who were not excelling in school. His teacher would elect him to be pusher of the wheelchairs. He felt important. However, I never really knew if he was working to his potential or if he was a good helper in class. I became room mother so I could see how he interacted with the other children. He made friends better than the older child, but never liked school. He attended two elementary schools before he graduated from the sixth grade. Speaking with the principal from the second school, I was informed that he was choosing friends that were not motivated in school activities.

"Mrs. K do you know what middle school you will be choosing for your son?" she asked.

"No, I haven't really given it thought. I suppose we will go to his home school," I replied.

"Have you ever thought about private school?" she said, as she lifted her eyebrows. As if she had a personal preference concerning his middle school years.

"I suppose I should try to look into the schools and see what is available," I continued.

"That might be a good idea. He is a follower and I think a private school would be a good way to get him interested in learning instead of socializing. A smaller classroom situation would be perfect for him. He is smart and I don't think he is giving all his potential to his class work," she admitted.

This information was a wake-up call for my husband and I. We talked about it several nights and then looked into three different private schools. It was already spring and the end of the school year, so I was starting to panic. What if we couldn't get him into a private school? How would I get him to the schools in our area? Private schools do not have buses. I was working and had to be at work before he went to school.

I took the day off and went to two schools. One was close by our house. It was a Baptist school and seemed very small. I watched the activities in the classrooms and walked the halls as the children changed classes. The children were disorderly and punishment seemed harsh. There was a waiting list and so this school did not seem to be an option.

Next I traveled thirty minutes to a downtown school that some of our church youth attended. Again I watched and read all about the school. The parents would take turns driving the kids, and I would only have to take off one or two days a month. I sat in the principal's office and questioned her about music and sports. They did not have programs that interested my son. They didn't have a lunch room and he would have to bring his own lunch. Somehow, this was not appealing to me. I just didn't like the school. No air conditioning, no lunchroom, and no special areas. What was I doing to my child?

Again I wanted to visit the public school near by and see what was going on there. I sat with the principal for about an hour. He gave me a picture of mass confusion. I was in the hall when the classes changed and was almost run over. The language was pathetic and there was no dress code at the time. It was exactly as I expected. Students were lined up in front of the office and a principle or teacher was screaming at them to tell the truth according to what they had witnessed.

After these visits I knew that I needed an answer and so I started to pray and look through the phone book. Each school Catholic, Protestant, and Traditional were all booked up for the coming year. There were an abundant number of kids born in that year and middle schools were expanding to satisfy the needs. Private schools had anticipated the need months ago and so the parents already attending were allowed to sign up their children months ahead. It was a hopeless situation and I was very upset for not realizing that I didn't see the need to plan for the next school year.

It was May and I needed to get this problem solved before it drove me crazy. I picked my son up from school and we took a little ride. I had seen this school in the phone book and didn't give it a second thought because it was fifteen miles away from my home. As we pulled up into the parking lot, a teacher was walking out of the school. I rolled down my window and asked her if she was a teacher. She acknowledged that she was the Librarian.

"Is this a good school?" I asked.

"Oh my yes," she replied.

"Does it have a band program?" I continued.

"Strange you should ask that question. We are starting a band next year. We have hired a band teacher for the music department. It's just the best school for students who are interested in continuing their education. Most of our students go on to college," she replied.

This was the first time any of the schools had addressed the issue of college education. My son had already told me that he didn't want to go to college because he hated school. Secretly I was hoping that this school could be the one to encourage him to feel good about himself and find out what he wanted to do after he graduated. I could just feel myself grinning inside.

"Do I need an appointment to visit the school or can I just go in there now?" I asked.

"What grade are you thinking about," she inquired.

"My son will be in the sixth grade, I wanted to get him in there for next year," I informed.

"Oh! You need to call right away. The sixth grade is full or almost full. Call first thing in the morning and tell them that you want to see the school," she stated.

I thanked her and turned to my son. I could see that he was mad that I would even consider the thought of going to a school where he would not know one person in his class. My heart was broken. What was I going to do?

I talked to my husband about the school. He informed me that it was fifteen miles away from home. He also informed me that we were not Baptist. Then there was the tuition to think about. How were we going to pay the tuition? I didn't even ask about the tuition. I was trying to figure out how I was going to be at work every day by eight-thirty. I owned a theater and my shows started at ten o'clock. That means that I would have to be there by eight-thirty to get the theater ready and make sure the props were set before the show. We always had phone calls at eight-thirty when teachers arrived at school. Someone had to be there to cover for me.

Still praying, I discussed this with my mother. She agreed that my son needed to be in a small setting. He was depressed and angry about something. I was not sure exactly what the problem could be but later figured it out. I have my own opinion but it will stay in my heart. Anyway, when I discussed this with my mother, she said she would help me pay for his tuition. I was encouraged and I just had to take a look inside the school to see what was going on in the classrooms.

I took the day off, at noon, after the morning show and drove out to the school. I had an appointment with the school adviser. When I walked into the school, it was so warm and friendly. I was escorted into an office and a young woman came in and introduced herself. She was kind and personable. She asked me what age child I wanted to enroll. When I said, a sixth grader, she frowned and continued to tell me that there was no room for that grade. I was so disappointed. Still she didn't rush me off. She gave me some papers to fill out and informed me that there may be students that don't show up or pull out.

"Just pray about it," she said as she placed the papers in my hand.

"I'll put your name and phone number on the list and if anything at all comes open I will call you," she explained.

"I'll show you around if you like," she continued.

"Oh wonderful, I would love to see the kids in action," I replied.

We walked the halls and stopped to watch teachers instruct students in reading, science, and mathematics. I could not believe my eyes. When the bell rang, I moved aside and the students excused themselves and quietly got books out of their lockers. Teachers were standing behind their classes as they picked up their belongings and lined up to walk down the stairs to their next classroom. The next set of students came and went the same way. Talking among themselves, and walking into the classrooms greeting friends without confusion or disorder. I sat in back of a classroom. I noticed each had put their homework on the desk waiting for some chosen student to collect the homework assignment. Then without notice I started to leave the room, the teacher asked the children who wanted to pray. One little girl stood up and said a prayer for the class and the teacher. I was totally blown away. In a time when we as teachers were not allowed to say the word 'prayer,' a child chooses to stand quietly at her desk and pray for her friends and teacher.

The school representative then took me up stairs to see the high school students. I expected to see the rowdy group of high school students as I walked up the stairs and entered the hallway. Instead, I saw students greeting the teachers and talking with staff as if they were friends. Lockers were again shutting and locks opening as locker buddies were standing quietly waiting to grab books and notes out for class. The classes were small, but larger than I expected. Fifteen to twenty in each room. The halls were clean of graffiti and the floor was clean enough to eat off of. I had not seen this in a public school without a threat or punishment from the staff or principal. I had worked for years in public schools and I supported public school. How could a school have so much order without threat or punishment? Students had a different kind of respect for each other as well as their teachers. The teachers were in the hall, waiting patiently for each student to assemble into the classroom.

Our next stop was the lunchroom. There were children filling their plates at a salad bar. Some of them were making sandwiches and warm plate lunches. The lunchroom was quiet and there were no lunchroom monitors keeping peace in the room. Just one individual helping guide students quietly to a table to enjoy their meal. Students were sitting with friends and talking quietly. I was amazed that lunch was like eating in a cafe.

Before I left I thanked the school representative that had escorted me throughout the school. She and I had already bonded. She was talking about her children and I was sharing stories about my kids. I was sure that God was giving me an answer I had longingly prayed for, even though there were no vacancies in the sixth grade.

We went back to her office and she urged me to fill out all the information and get it back to her soon.

"If you could get this back to me by tomorrow, I will have to put your application on top. Not all the people waiting for a placement have the information needed to grant them an interview with the head master," she explained.

I thanked her and hurried to my car. I looked over the information and noticed that I needed his grades from school, a letter from our church and reference letters from friends and teachers. I went to my son's school to get information needed from his teacher. I knew the school secretary personally. I asked her if she could give the school application to his teacher. I told her how important it was to have the papers back by the next day. She was happy to do me a favor and I informed her that I would be back the next morning. I didn't know if she would be willing to fill out the papers so soon but it was a chance I had to take. I stopped by the councilor's office and asked for a copy of his records. Fortunately she was not busy and had time to pull his file and make me a copy. Then I called my teacher friend that was his kindergarten teacher and a close friend of both of my children. She agreed to write a letter of recommendation. I drove to our church and had his youth minister write a letter of recommendation and left one for our minister. Each one promised me that I could pick up their letters before noon the next day.

Everything was set, but I didn't ask about the tuition. I called the school back and talked about the tuition. How much did I need to put down before next year. I learned that I could pay in three installment plans. I then went to my bank book and noticed that I could handle the first part of the tuition. I prayed and prayed that day. Please, God, I need to get my son into this school. If it is your will show me what to do next. This may sound like a selfish prayer, but I do believe that God needs to know that we are willing to be obedient. Sometimes we need to be taxed to the max personally to achieve what we desire spiritually, even if he has already willed it for the future.

I discussed the time and distance with my husband that night. I told him about the school and how I strongly believed that it was God's will that we put our son in this school. Then we filled out the information together in hopes that we were doing what was right. My husband could not believe the questions on the entrance form.

"These are very personal questions. Do we have to answer all of these questions?" he asked.

"Yes, we do. So come on, go to the next one," I fussed.

"How long have we been married? How do we feel about marriage? Gee, on the next page they will be asking us how many times we've had sex," he laughed.

"No, they save that question for the interview," I explained.

After filling out the information, I wrote a check and went to bed. The next morning I made all the stops to pick up the questions from the school and church. To my amazement everyone had filled out the information and that would complete the paper work. Then I went back to work and talked to my employees. I asked the office assistant if she could start coming into work at eight-thirty next year. To my surprise, she reminded me that her son would now be going to high-school and would be driving her younger son. Perfect! This was all working out, but I still need a spot in the class. I needed someone to drop out of school. Should I pray for that?

I took all the paper work and drove out to the school. I was greeted by the office secretary and she took my papers. She promised me that they would get it in the right hands. I asked if she could check the information and see if they had what they needed for an interview. She looked over the paperwork and said that everything looked ready. I remember it was on a Friday, so I had all weekend to pray about this decision. I also worked on my son telling him about the school and how wonderful it was. He played the saxophone and so I reminded him that he could take band. That encouraged him, but he was still upset that he may not know anyone there. I prayed at church and I called my mom and sister to pray with me. I suppose all three of us prayed night and day.

Monday I had a show and went to work like usual. I was still praying and never thought about another school. I stopped calling private schools and never visited another middle school. Later that week I got a phone call. Just what I had been waiting for.

"Mrs. K. we just had a student drop out of the sixth grade for next year. We do have a waiting list, but since you have all your papers in order and have paid down the money, I am going to go ahead and set up your interview with the headmaster," she informed me.

"Wonderful! Thank you," I excitedly replied.

I made an appointment on Thursday so my husband and I could go together to the interview. I was very nervous and we decided that this was up to God. We agreed to let this be the deciding factor for putting our son in this particular school. We were not Baptist and we felt that they would probably ask us questions about the Baptist faith. We were going to be honest and just tell them how we felt about Christianity. We were not going to join the church and give extra to the church. This was strictly about the school, the values and the education of our child.

When we walked into the office everything was very professional. We were asked about discipline, philosophy of education and how we felt about our child attending chapel there at school. I answered the education questions and the

Headmaster kept looking at my husband. We were shocked that he never looked to me for answers. Later we learned that the man of the house was the one who was supposed to take charge and make decisions. We were compartmentalized at our house. My husband paid the bills; I took care of the house and the kids. He never went to conferences that were usually in the middle of the day and most of the time I did all the discipline because I was home when fights broke out and punishments were handed down.

Oops! I suppose that we were not the normal couple. For one thing I worked. I had always worked, and never really knew of a woman or mother of any value that didn't work. My mother always worked and she took care of thousands of children who had working mothers. I always felt that mothers that didn't work just did not care about themselves or their family. I went to school to get an education so I could help my husband pay for the things in life that we needed. He never asked me not to work and I never thought it was a bad thing to work. Now I see and hear that Christian mother's stay at home and even home school. They believe that the family develops values. They are physically and mentally nourished while the mother sets positive examples from the Bible. These children are disciplined with love and will become better students that grow to be physically, mentally, and morally complete.

Wow was I wrong. I came from a dysfunctional family. My parents were divorced when I was three. My mother remarried when I was five and I started to work in the family business at the age of ten. If you did not work and do chores in our family, you were called lazy and were punished. There is a big difference between punishment and discipline. Love was when you gave pleasure to your parents by obeying them and completing chores without being asked. Love was receiving a box of candy, a new skirt, or maybe a shopping trip downtown. We went to church every Sunday, never read our Bible and invited over the minister for Sunday lunch. We gave to those in need, washed cars to earn money for youth group and went to church revivals every night when evangelists visited our church. If we had sinned we knew that we should go to the altar and confess our sins on Sundays.

As we walked to the car, I realized that I never had a chance with this Headmaster. I said all the wrong things. I never prayed with my children and my husband never prayed with the family. We didn't know the Bible. We spent our church life with other families like ours, who socialized at ballgames and Sunday school outings. Our children were baptized and accepted Christ, but I dare say they could not name the books of the Bible. We seldom missed church and always gave an offering. I thought we were wonderful parents, doing all the right things according to God's will. I was the director of the children's choir and my husband worked with me every Sunday morning teaching children's church. We were involved with the nursing home church service once a month and helped down at the mission serving homeless people once a month.

We left our children with our parents often and they rewarded them with gifts and money just because they were grandchildren. I was even chastised for not rewarding the children when they made good grades. Each child got a dollar for each A that was on their report card. My children were always on the honor roll so they made good money on report card days.

I truly believe that we blew it. I should have kept my mouth shut. I should have let my husband do all the talking. I just didn't know. We worried all the way home. We were not sure why we blew it, but later one of the members explained that the Bible gives instructions to married couples and suggest certain ways to lead the family.

It was a week or so before we heard from the school. I was totally taking responsibility for the lack of family structure. I had a hard time trying to figure out what we did together as a family. My husband couldn't think of anything either. I spent a long hard week trying to think about where we went wrong.

Then one day at work I got a call from the school. The voice of the other end of the phone informed me that my son was accepted into the school. I was so elated to get this news. My son on the other hand was not happy. It took me a whole summer to try to convince him that he would love his new school. Soon I would learn that it would be best not to mention it until it was time for school to start. We had to buy uniforms. He hated the experience. He would only wear the tan pants and the blue shirt. He did not want to wear a sweater or stripped shirt. It was definitely a struggle. Again I prayed asking God to send him a friend at school.

Each day he complained about going to school. He didn't want to get out of the car. He was angry at me and the teachers at school. He was convinced that no one liked him. He got in trouble for fighting on the playground. Again I never stopped praying. God, there must be a reason for us putting my child in this school. Why did we go through all the paperwork and interview if we are going to put him back into public school? Every time I prayed I would still feel the tug at my heart that something good was going to happen. I drove thirty miles daily to take him to school and pick him up from school. Then little by little my prayers were being answered. He was making friends and talking about other children. He liked the lunches and liked the fact that he could drink juice instead of milk. He had a crush on a little girl in music and they would walk out of school together. I thought we were making progress, but she was older than he and of course broke his heart.

The next year he made more friends and even asked a friend to go on vacation with us to the beach. Still I prayed for his happiness. There were times when he would regress and I would start praying that I would see more changes. When I picked him up from school, he would be angry and mean with me. He didn't like the idea that I had to drop him off at home and go back to work. Some days I had to take him with me to teach afterschool drama. He was so shy, he would stay in the car and do his homework. By the end of his second year he made friends with several boys. He was inviting them over on weekends and having sleepovers that would involve playing instruments in our basement. They even formed a band and preformed on stage at a local theater. We had parties at our house and took a group of his friends to the beach. I was seeing God answering my prayers slowly, but in his time.

Then one year, the will of God hit me in the face. My son was chosen to sing with the all county choir, along with three or four other students. One student was the Principal's daughter. He was excused from school for three days and worked solely at The University of Louisville Music department with a talented director. He learned to sing parts and sing in French. He was totally taken away with the talent of the other students singing with him in the choir. One girl was his favorite. I soon learned that she was beautiful and that she was the Principal's daughter. She did not attend school there all day, but only came for music. They talked daily and enjoyed each others company whenever they could meet at parties or school events.

His senior year was the happiest year. He was in love with this young woman. Her parents and I thought that it was just a phase. We let them see each other occasionally and tried to treat it as just friends. After graduation, I noticed that every conversation had her name in it. We teased him but it didn't make him angry. He shared his feelings about her with me and I would tell him that it was great that he had a girlfriend. However, he still had to get his education. He didn't want to leave home to go to school. He wanted to stay home close to his girlfriend. He was so much in love with her that he started visiting her at collage. She was a music major living on campus at Boyce School (located at the Baptist Seminary). Together they hung out with friends and studied the Gospel. He became a regular at her house and her family fell in love with him. She visited us often and we accepted her as family. He was so motivated to finish school and get a job that he went straight through school without taking a summer vacation.

He was praying about their relationship and sharing his love of the word with her father, who was a minister. He wanted to know if it was in God's will to marry this beautiful girl. He soon found that he could not finish his day without talking with her on the phone to say goodnight. They sang together and played musical instruments together. It was a sure thing that they were in love. They dated for five years and the month after he graduated from college he asked her to marry him. That summer they were married and today I have the happiest son in the whole world. This was truly a divine intervention. This son, who was saved by an angel on the basement stairs, is now sharing his faith with others and working in church. There is no doubt in my mind that God has big plans for this couple.

You may not believe my stories. That is totally up to you. I would have no reason to share this book with you if I felt that I was not sharing the truth. There are many skeptic people who think that Christians are over the top. We make something out of nothing just to give us an opportunity to make others believe in God. That may be true. However, Jesus was over the top. When he healed the sick and turned the water into wine, I am sure there were people who saw it with their own eyes and still failed to believe that he was real.

DIVINE INTERVENTIONS

You must understand that God doesn't always like the thoughts of the unbeliever, but He still loves the unbeliever and hears his prayers. The Bible also tells us to pray in earnest and be sincere when we ask the Father for something special.

Remember the following:
1. God is all powerful. He is the only one who can make something out of nothing.
2. God has a purpose and plan for your life.
3. God will never ever leave you alone.

These are gifts that he gives to the believers. He also gives us his word in the Bible. If you feel that you don't understand what the Bible is saying to you, then you might want to buy a study Bible that explains clearly each verse that is written. Read a verse or two everyday, share with other believers. Surround your life with positive convicted believers. Soon you will be noticing that there are divine interventions and you will not ask if it is real or how it happened. You will be swift to share it with others.

Christians in Trouble: Why Does God Let Bad Things Happen to Good People?

How many times have you asked this question? This is a question that many ministers get from families that lose loved ones or struggle with life crises. First God wants good things for his children. He does not plan to destroy us. Sometimes bad things come into our lives, because we allow sin to take over our sinful nature. I have asked this question myself. I can honestly say that sometimes people can be blessed by the life lesson that God presents in bad situations.

It is my opinion that God has his own way to shake us up before we give in and listen to his divine will. Sometimes we are like children. We forget the past burn or hurt and turn around and sin the same sin repeatedly. We forget that we are hurting others in our lives that truly love us. This also goes for the person who is always helping the down and out because that is what we think God wants us to do. When things don't turn out the way we plan, then we start to question God. Maybe it was not in God's plan for me to be involved in solving the problem. This is why it is so important to listen to the enter spirit.

When the spirit of God knocks at your heart, you will feel the urgency to help someone by stepping out of your comfort zone. That is what we need to feel when God uses us to do his work. To me it feels like an urgent desire that I cannot stop. The desire does not go away. You think about the situation every minute of the day. You pray for someone and you still have that feeling that you need to connect spiritually. Then you make the phone call or send a card of encouragement and you know just what to say. That is when you realize that God has used you to care about another person or make a difference in a situation.

We must remember that we are not God and we cannot second guess his decisions. Maybe God allows bad things in our life, so we will stumble repeatedly until we learn that this decision does not give me inner peace and joy that comes when I pray for God's guidance. Remember that sometimes trials test our faith. How far will we go before we wake up and trust that God will always be in control?

Recently I have learned that a divine intervention can come from strife and frustration. In my situation I have learned that it is true that knowledge comes with age. It has always been my nature to help everyone in need. If I could fix something, give something, or lend something to someone who needed my help, I would jump right up and volunteer my services. In the last fifteen years, I have made and lost many so-called friends because I tried to fix their problems and save them from despair. Little did I realize that some people like to make friends by being the victim.

I have tried to protect an employee from spousal abuse, and housed a homeless family of five in my basement for two months. I have paid for marriage counseling and babysit for couples who needed a weekend away. I have made supper for friends and bought diapers and milk for babies. I have paid employees when they said they were too sick to show up for work. I have rented out property and allowed renters, who were friends, to pay late, only to find out that they would leave without notice and with property that belonged to the house. I have washed clothes and cleaned house for friends who could not afford the time. I have provided beds for families who were sleeping on the floor.

I have given away furniture and volunteered my time away from my own family to work in a friends business without pay. All of this and I have not even mentioned the money my husband and I have lent to others that we will never see again. We were embezzled from and have lost enough money to buy a new home. For eight years we trusted a person, who was posing as a Christian, to run his front office. We had a hard time understanding why she was stealing great amounts of money from the business and lying to friends and associates.

I write about all of these people not because I want the praise and glory – I praise God that I had the funds to help others. I also think God wants us to beware of people who take advantage of good people with funds. In return, I was left broken hearted, snubbed, and rejected. I had to learn that the devil is alive and he will test you and try your faith. I know that God put these people in my life for some reason. I might have been the only person God could use to give hope to others. Maybe He wanted me to wake up and see that people are not always who you think they are. I only know that when you give in His name He sees that you had good intentions and He will bless you as you learn from each situation.

I was upset each time I lost contact with each of these dishonest friends. Somehow I would always feel that it was my fault that we stopped talking or ended our friendship. I could not realize that people who claim to be Christians could lie, cheat and steal from others. How could this be? They attended church and talked the talk. Then God took these people out of my life and gave me a huge intervention.

I started attending Bible study with true Christian friends. I became wise when I learned that the Bible warns of false profits. I learned that God took these people out of my life for a reason. I had to learn the hard way that there are few people who know what God says about living the Christian life. There are fewer people who care about hurting others. It has surprised me that most people do not care about the welfare of their neighbors. Where are the true Christians? Some are sitting in church as pretenders. Learn how a real Christian lives for Christ. Study the Bible and don't expect something for your time, love and generosity given to others. Remember that Christ owned nothing. He gave us so much, yet when he left this world, he had no belongings, and he too was deceived by his friends. This thought gives me hope.

A Little Child Will Lead: Don't be Afraid to Share Your Story

If you have ever taught in a kindergarten class, you can agree with me, that children love show and tell. A day when they get the chance to stand in front of their peers and tell or show something wonderful that only they know about. Rarely do children miss school on the day of show and tell. Whatever happened exciting at home will definitely be a part of the circle time at show and tell.

I remember one child told us that her parents went to the *Funny Farm* and she got to stay with her favorite babysitter. I had only heard the crazy house or mental hospital called the *Funny Farm*. I knew this was going to be good, so I started questioning her.

"So why did your parents go to the *Funny Farm*?" I asked.

"I am not sure, but they were really excited and dressed up. My mom said for us kids to be good because she had been waiting a long time to have a night out."

"Were you good?" I asked.

"Of course," she explained, "and my favorite babysitter came and stayed with us."

"She had also been to the *Funny Farm*."

"Where is the *Funny Farm*?" I asked.

"I don't know but you can ask my mom when she comes to get me today."

"So she is out?" I questioned.

"Sure, she brought me to school today."

With this I decided to stop my questions and go on to the next child.

That afternoon I found out that there was a new comedy club in town and it was called *"The Funny Farm."* You can see why I also enjoyed show and tell. I learned a lot about each child when they shared stories concerning home and friends. I have seen all kinds of personal items snuck into back packs to be shared with the class. Oh if we could only have the honesty of a little child. They are like little sponges soaking up everything they see and hear.

I met Chuck at the Trading Post Mall one morning. He stopped to speak and we talked about people being out of work. I told him my husband was out of work, and he said, "God bless you. God must have something special planned for your husband. He won't be out of work long."

Then I told him that we were retired and worked at the Trading Post. I also told him that we were Christians and believed that God has something good in store for us. We talked for a few minutes and Chuck began to share his life with us.

Chuck was in his thirties. He related that he spent years on drugs and alcohol. Then one day he went into rehab where someone shared Jesus with him. He learned that the only way to stay sober was to stay in the word and let God be a part of his life. Chuck was with his beautiful wife who also came from a dysfunctional family and together they shared this story.

It is a blessing that Chuck and Kim can share with their daughter the love of Jesus and prayer. The home of Chuck and Kim is now open to praying and reading the Bible. The family goes to church together and shares with friends their love and personal relationship with Christ. It was Jennifer their daughter who made the intervention that persuaded Chuck to change the life of his neighbor.

Like most kids, Jennifer loved being outside and around the children in her neighborhood. Kim always made sure she knew where Jennifer was going and who she was with. On this summer day, Jennifer was curious about the amount of cars parked in front of Joe's house. Seeing Joe's granddaughter on the porch, she started her investigation.

"Hi Angie, what's going on in the house?" she asked.

"It's my grandfather," replied Angie. "He is very sick and might die. The doctors say he has cancer and he has to take some shots or something."

"It sounds like everyone inside there is arguing or yelling about something," said Jennifer as she nestled up against the screen window trying to take a peek inside the room.

"No," said Angie. "They just want him to go to the hospital and take some shots or something. Grandpa doesn't want to take anymore medicine. He said that he is ready to die and then everyone started telling him what to do. It was making me sad so I just left and came out here."

"Oh my Angie, we should put him on our prayer list," remarked Jennifer.

"Prayer list?" questioned Angie. "How will that help him?"

"Well, sometimes when we ask Jesus to fix something he will do it. We pray for sick people a lot at church," said Jennifer.

"Do you think he will die?" asked Jennifer.

"He can't eat much and he sleeps all the time. I just wish he would be like he used to be," continued Angie. "I don't want him to die." She snuffed as she sat on the porch swing trying not to let Jennifer see her tears.

"He's going to be fine Angie. Even if he dies, he will be in heaven with Jesus," continued Jennifer.

"Does he know about Jesus?" asked Jennifer.

"I don't know," said Angie, "he doesn't go to church like you and your family."

"He says Jesus when something happens but, I don't think he is praying."

"You mean he swears?" replied Jennifer.

"Swears? What is that, Jennifer?"

"It says in the Bible that you should not take the name of Jesus in vain. I think that means call his name when you hit your thumb or fall off of your bike. I really don't know, I will ask my father. He says that we call upon Jesus only when we are praying or talking about him. It's somewhere in the Bible."

"Do you want me to tell everyone at church to pray for him?" continued Jennifer.

"I guess so if you think it would help," answered Angie.

"It will help," said Jennifer as she peeked in the window one more time and then jumped off the porch.

"I'll tell my father to pray for him. He is a good prayer. See you later," said Jennifer as she ran down the street and climbed the steps to her house.

Jennifer went through the house looking for her father. Chuck was in the garage and when he saw Jennifer running he knew she had something important to talk to him about.

"Daddy, can you stop what you are doing right now," asked Jennifer.

"What is going on girl? You're out of breath," said Chuck as he grabbed his long tall ten year old daughter up into his arms and twirled her around.

"Daddy, did you know that Mr. Grimes is going to die?" replied Jennifer.

"I knew he had been in the hospital. What is wrong with him," asked Chuck.

"Cancer!" answered Jennifer. "He doesn't want to take anymore medicine and the whole family is down there trying to get him to go back to the hospital and get more shots. He says he wants to die."

"Should we put him on our prayer list at church?" asked Jennifer.

Chuck had lived down the street from Joe for several years. He knew Joe was not a Christian and that he hated it when Chuck started going to church and talking about religion.

Joe was the Godfather of the neighborhood. He was always fixing cars and helping people out who needed something moved. He was retired from his job, so he enjoyed being needed in the neighborhood. Now in his sixties, he was a father to the guys Chuck's age and a grandfather to their children. He knew everything about everyone on the street. He loved animals and volunteered to take care of dogs and cats when people went on vacation. He wasn't rich but he loved being home with his wife and always invited his friends in for a drink and a piece of advice. He was one of those kind of men that you enjoyed being around. He always had a joke for you or shared a story. He never wore anything but jeans and a tee shirt.

Chuck needed to talk to Joe. He told his daughter to go into the house and stay with her mother. Then he walked down the street and up onto Joe's porch. He could tell by the cars in the drive that all of his sons and daughters were visiting. Without knocking, Chuck opened up the front door and walked right into the living room. He spoke to the grandchildren sitting on the couch watching TV. Then he made his way down the hall to the bedroom where everyone was camped out in the hall and around the bed. His wife looked up at me and told Joe that I was visiting.

"Joe, look up, Chuck is here to see you," said his wife.

"Hi Joe, looks like you are trying to take a little nap," Chuck remarked.

"No, Chuck I just think that I am at the end of my time. I am tired of feeling like this and if I have to spend the rest of my life in bed I might as well die. That chemo treatment hasn't done one bit of good. It makes me sick and I am not going back into the hospital. It ain't gonna do no good," replied Joe.

"Well, maybe we should just pray Joe. What do you think," asked Chuck.

"Don't go trying that religious stuff on me. I don't want to hear it," said Joe.

"Joe, you are the one that said you wanted to die. So if you are thinking about dying, then you have to face the facts," reminded Chuck.

"No! Chuck if you start talking about Jesus and stuff you can just go on back home," replied Joe.

"I love you Joe. I want to see you again someday." Said Chuck, as he walked toward the bed and pushed his way between the bed and Joe's wife.

"What if you do die? Where would you go?" Chuck asked.

"Don't know and don't care," said Joe.

Now all of Joe's children were pushing back into the room and watching Joe react to Chuck. None of Joe's family had ever gone to church or claimed to be of any kind of religion. Chuck had been friends with them since childhood. He knew that he was totally on his own in this area.

When Chuck turned around to walk away, his feet would not move. He noticed the familiar faces of Chuck's sons and still he saw fear instead of anger. Then he turned back around to face Joe.

"Joe, it doesn't matter if you take the chemotherapy now and live a few more years or if you decide that you just want to go ahead and die. It's a fact that you are going to die someday. I just want you to understand that when you die, you have two choices: heaven or hell. If you accept Christ into your life he will be standing there in front of you with his arms open and he will say come on home Joe." Then Chuck turned around to the family.

"We are all going to die someday. Do you believe in Jesus?" asked Chuck. "If you don't believe in Jesus then you have no choice but to go to hell. This is a place where you will suffer the rest of your days. There really is a hell and it is mentioned in the Bible."

It was now very quite in the house where ten to fifteen people were previously cussing and arguing Joe's case. Chuck continued to witness to the group. Turning to Joe, Chuck went on to speak.

"You like to gamble, play cards, and the lottery. I am just asking all of you, what would it hurt to take one more chance and accept Jesus into your heart? This is a sure thing. What do you have to lose? If you say yes, you win a trip to Heaven. A wonderful life and a chance to be with each other the rest of your life."

"Now Chuck, I am not a good person and I can't do that religious stuff," replied Joe.

"I know that Joe, and so does Jesus, but guess what? He is going to love you anyway. He wants you just as you are. You don't have to do anything special but just accept him into your heart and share his love with others. Do you think you can do that?" asked Chuck.

Joe started to cry. "I already love everyone. I am just afraid to say yes."

"Don't be afraid of God, he already knows that you are a sinner and I am a sinner and he wants to fix us before we die. He wants you and your family here to read the Bible and learn why he loves you and how you can change before you die. Will you think about what I am saying and let me pray with you and your family?" asked Chuck.

Joe looked up at his wife, she was turned toward the window, and tears were streaming down her face. Chuck knew she was having a hard time accepting the cancer that was taking over her husband's body. Chuck turned Lee Ann around and took her hand in his.

"Lee Ann, can I pray with your family?" asked Chuck

Lee Ann shook her head yes as she grabbed her husband's hand and watched as each one of their children grabbed hands and gathered around the bed.

Chuck started to pray. He prayed for Joe and his health and the decision he was going to make at the doctor's office. He prayed for Lee Ann and for each of the family members. The longer he prayed the more tears flowed in that small bedroom and hallway. Joe agreed to accept Christ into his heart. One after another the family fell to their knees and prayed to accept Jesus. The spirit of the Lord was truly there and everyone felt something wonderful as they turned to one another to say, "I am sorry."

Chuck phoned his wife and she came to the house. She gave a witness of what Christ had done in her life. How he had taken her out of a broken home where there was alcohol and abuse. She quoted scripture from her Bible. She explained that this was Jesus' words written in the Bible just for us. Then she encouraged everyone to get a Bible of their own.

Kim, Chuck's wife, told me that it was a miracle that each person stopped to listen. She explained that some family members want to go to church with her and Chuck.

"Joe's family are changed people. It was something to watch as the Holy Spirit took over the bodies of each person in that room," said Kim.

"What about Joe," I asked. "Did he die?"

"Three weeks later. He continued to take the chemotherapy, but he lived just three more weeks." Said Kim

"We went to the funeral home and everyone there was stopping us to thank us for telling them about Jesus," shared Chuck.

"Some of the family spoke at the funeral and told the friends and relatives about that afternoon when Joe decided he wanted to meet Jesus when he died. All of this because of little Jennifer. I would have never known he was that close to death had Jennifer not asked me to pray for her friend Joe. I feel that God used Jennifer to go to the house when all the family was gathered in front of Joe to make a decision about his health. What was the chance of me getting the attention of the whole family at one time?" said Chuck as he shook his head.

"Never!" he explained. "Never!"

I asked Chuck if I could use his story for my book _Divine Interventions_. He smiled at me and quickly accepted my offer. Then he prayed with me, my husband, and my sister.

"It was wonderful to meet you today he said," as he grabbed his wife's hand and continued through the mall. Then Chuck turned around and yelled back to me.

"My wife didn't want to go shopping here, but I felt very strongly about coming to this mall. I now know why," said Chuck.

We both said together, "It was a divine intervention."

I could not have shared Chuck's story if we had not met at the mall.

Thank you God for this simple intervention.

God Promises to Protect His People: How Should We Pray?

I believe that God enjoys protecting his people. Those who love Him and continually pray for His love and guidance. Those of us who recognize that God is behind the divine in divine interventions. Once we pray and ask God for help, he immediately hears our prayers and goes to work trying to provide ways to work out our problems. When we fail to believe in prayers and divine answers, I also believe that God will let you do it on your own. I believe this because of the story written in the Bible. The people of Israel were forbidden to inherit the Promise Land because they stopped believing in God (Hebrews. 3:15-19).

The Lord was providing for the needs of the Israelites as he had promised. However, it was not quick enough or good enough. There was constant complaining and disbelief. When we begin to speak out about our disbelief then it says to God, "I don't believe you can help me." You are just setting yourselves up for the enemy's attack. Daily prayer insures that God knows your needs and knows that you are sincere about the problem you pray about.

I have since learned that I can pray for a divine intervention. Why not? I have seen so many in my life and people continue to share their interventions with me. So why can't I pray for a divine intervention? Not a selfish pray, for God does not want us to be arrogant and selfish. It's not about us – it's all about Him.

The biggest and best intervention that I have not yet mentioned in my book is my prayer for a Godly marriage. I should say it was one of the most important interventions of my life. I am sure that my husband would agree. However, there are times we have been walking in storms whirling our marriage around like a tornado that has the potential to destroy. I am sure the devil smiles each time this storm approaches our marriage. Still my husband reminds me that we were put together for a reason and we will get through this together. On the other hand, I scream, "I don't care! He didn't see this coming, and we have nothing in common." I try to find every excuse under the sun to make my anger and rage sound official.

We must remember that we are human and we will follow the feeling that society allows us to have. We all try to measure our marriage, our spouses and our families against standards set by the world. Remember, if we are in the world and doing what the world expects from us, we cannot be in God's Word. I must admit it is so much easier to follow the world and do what we want. It's easier not to get involved with people who are believers. It's easier not to read the Bible and study God's word. It's easier to lie and cheat to get what we want. But it is much harder to regret. When you know the difference between right and wrong, I feel that we start down the road of remorse and regret. I can't live there and I refuse to stay there. Although I regret many things in my life, I know that these things are in the past and God has already forgiven me for my past. When I turn back, I hear God's voice say, "Move on, sister."

1982 My Marriage:
I was twenty-eight years old and still looking for love in all the wrong places. I thought attending church would be fruitful, but failed to see that there are false believers setting in churches. I attended Lay Mission weekends and visited Christian fellowship groups. I learned not to put much faith into guys who promise to call you and ask you out. They never call much-less remember your name. I played tennis, visited single bars and attended parties. This was not for me. I hated the single world. I just wanted to meet someone who was honest and wanted to attend church with me. Someone who would like my family and enjoy attending family actives. Someone who wasn't too drunk to take me home. Someone who loved me for who I was, not for what I was. I had finished college and was serious about teaching.

One Saturday afternoon I was invited to a wedding. I hated weddings but I went anyway. I sat in the pew and watched as the singer took his place in front of the church. Without a doubt, that was the best singer, I had ever heard. His voice was low and his song was so meaningful. For some reason my attention was totally fixed on this song and singer. It had meaning for me. It was as though the Spirit was tugging at my heart. The name of the song was, *"One in a Million."*

I had never heard that song before although it was popular on the radio back in 1980. One line of the song says, "God showed compassion and sent to me a one in a million: you." That song stayed in my head the rest of the day. I don't remember much more about the service but I had to find that song. That night as I sat in my small one bedroom apartment, I started to pray.

"God, is there really one person out of a million out there that you have set aside for me? If there is, then show me. I am asking for you to send me someone to love me. Someone that will take care of me and enjoy my life with me. Please God, bring him into my life. I am tired of all the guys who will not commit to a relationship. I will now leave this in your hands. If it is your will God show me what to do."

After I prayed, I took a pen and paper and started to write all the things I was feeling. I wrote until I had several pages of notes and thoughts. It was now about four in the morning and as I read over my feelings, I knew that I was serious about my prayer. I was willing to listen to what God wanted me to do. The first thing God wanted was for me to stop worrying about my future. I needed to focus on my job. Being a first year teacher, I was sure that I would get the ax at the end of the year. Louisville had too many teachers graduating from school that year and we were all looking for jobs. I was lucky that I was hired in the middle of the year when I graduated from college. I was also working on my master's degree so I needed time to go to school and be the best teacher I could so my evaluation would help me get a job in one of the local schools.

After that prayer, I felt that a burden was lifted from my heart. I thought I was already in love, but the guy I was in love with did not meet my standards or God's standards. Secretly I was hoping that God was going to change him and bring him into my life. He would be so much in love with me that I could not stop him from asking me to get married and moving in with him.

I waited for his stampede toward my apartment. I waited for him to call me and ask me that all important question. We saw each other often but I could tell that being married was not going to work. If we were going to get married, God had to do some major surgery on this relationship. Still I did not worry. I was not depressed anymore and I started enjoying life and my career.

It had almost been a year since I had prayed my sincere prayer for God to help me find a Christian husband. I had been on a trip to Hawaii and went to my friend's house to show her my pictures. During my visit, she mentioned something about a wonderful guy who lived next door. She asked me if I remembered him from high school. I did and I remembered that he was very popular. She continued to tell me he was a dentist, went to the Methodist church and wanted to meet a nice girl. I was Methodist and one year younger and so I said, "Well, just give him my number." I really didn't think she was serious, but a month later, he called me and we went on a blind date.

We became friends before we figured out that we were in love. He went to church with me and I went to church with him. We knew the same people and we had lived just blocks from each other all of our lives. We enjoyed the same music and watching movies. Before long he was a permanent fixture at my family events. My family loved him and his family loved me. It was a given that we belonged together and a year later we were married and he moved into my apartment.

Together we promised God to be faithful to him and train our children in a Christian home. We were just Sunday Christians until we started studying the Word. We started learning what we needed to make God the biggest and best part of our lives. We grew in our faith and continued to grow as we anticipate helping to parent our grandchildren.

Was This a Coincidence or a Divine Intervention? How Strong is Your Belief of Divine Intervention?

Recently a baby fell off of a hotel balcony several feet above the sidewalk below. As the mother stood leaning over the rails helplessly screaming and praying, the impossible happened. A woman sitting by the pool heard her screams and rushed to the sidewalk. She held up her hands and the baby fell into the stranger's arms. Within minutes the baby was safely returned to its mother. The local reporters are calling it an Easter miracle. The woman said she just happened to be in the right place at the right time. I call it a divine intervention willed by prayer and God.

Prayer is so powerful. If only we would just turn to prayer daily to communicate our needs to God. The Bible tells us that God knows our needs before we ask, but he wants us to come to him and trust in him. There are small things that we could pray about instead of worrying. Still, we fail to ask God for help. We forget that nothing is too small for God. God wants us to be happy here on earth just as he tells us about the happiness we will have in Heaven.

Most of us have repeated the Lord's prayer at sometime in our lives. While writing this book I realized that one of the important phrases in that prayer sums up God's purpose for all humans that roam the earth.

"Thy will be done, on earth as it is in Heaven."

God wants us to enjoy our lives here on earth as we anticipate our home in heaven. If we don't praise and enjoy God here on earth, then we won't really enjoy the life he has designed for us in Heaven. A life without pain, grief, unhappiness, problems, hunger, or disappointment. All I can say about this description is "Wow!"

Why can't this perfect world exist here on earth? The answer is sin.

It's because we live in a sinful world. A world that is taken over by Satan. We believe what people tell us instead of what God would have us to believe. We follow the trends of the world and accept what the world says about being right or wrong. When someone falls or fails we are all quick to judge.

We gossip with others by saying the following:

"Oh yes and he is a good Christian."

"He is one of those churchgoers."

Nonbelievers think that religion is the way to worship. You go to church, say a prayer or two, volunteer for Bible School, and attend all the services. Give money on a weekly basis, because the only reason the church needs people is for the money. Now we belong to the church. I am a Christian and that gives me the right to judge others.

Next we judge our friends and neighbors by the cars they drive the schools they attend and the clothes they wear. We join groups that will give us status, and we fill our lives with sinful entertainment that does not honor God.

"What's wrong with that," we say to ourselves.

"I am still a Christian because I go to church and ask for forgiveness," we say. "I help others and work for God when I can. I was baptized in the church and that makes me a member of God's family and a Christian."

Right?

No! God wants all of you.

The only person who gets to judge is God. "The Great I Am."

(Exodus 3:14) *I am who I am.*

Even if you never step inside a church door or give another penny you can still have a real relationship with God. Communicate with him daily and above all read his word so you know more about God and why he accepts you just the way you are.

When you come to the realization that you are one of his believers, He will use you in so many ways. You may be used for a divine intervention. You will definitely know that you are one of God's children and you will desire to be with other believers. When you feel the Spirit of God speak to your heart, you will find that you will have the desire to give time and money to help those in need.

Let's just face the facts. Satan is living everywhere we go. He is in a constant fight with the Holy Spirit of God. Satan will only bring us pleasure that will destroy our lives and allow us to live a lie. If we understand this, then we can understand why God places us in situations where we can show others that God is in control. We must admit that God is divine and that he will intervene when there is trouble and we call upon Him for help. He will send his angels to intercede for Him, and God will take care of problems that take the joy out of our lives. He will give us joy by promising us everlasting life.

Remember to call upon the Lord in times of trouble and believe that God will intervene when things are out of our control. When our car stalls on the expressway, when our kids get sick or badly hurt, when we are helpless and feel that there is noting left to solve the most difficult problems that may face us in this con-strife world where we live. Pray, pray, and pray some more. Next sit back and watch as God will intervene with his divine solutions. Like the Little Engine That Could, push forward and make it over the mountain. Believe that there are answers on the other side but don't stop to rest when one problem has been solved. Just know that there will always be bumps in the road. The next bump will be easier because you have seen with your own eyes that you can and will make it.

I sit here writing this book with several bumps in front of me. I have been very low and confused in the last few months. My children are all grown, my husband and I have retired and one would think that we have nothing to do but enjoy the last few years that God has given us. If this was so, then we would be in Heaven and not here in this broken sinful world.

The economy is bad. The property we own is not selling. The people who we trusted to secure our retirement funds have falsely represented their companies and our children are living life so fast that they have no time for themselves not to mention their poor old boring parents.

I expected to travel whenever we wanted. I anticipated it would be like it was in the fifties. We would see our children and grandchildren on Sundays. Everyone would be excited to be together. We would sit on the porch and make ice cream or cut a fresh watermelon with the neighbors. It was fun for us, why isn't it fun for them?

It's easy to build a negative environment when you put yourself and your wants first. God doesn't promise us a make-believe world.

To be honest, we don't even know our neighbors well enough to ask them to join our family on the front porch for watermelon. It's only half a mile down the street to Dairy Queen, and our kids don't enjoy just sitting on the porch with us without being entertained. Things have surly changed and as a baby boomer, I need to wake up and get with the times. I need to use my privilege of being a senior citizen to get a discount on ice cream. Forget the watermelon; it only rots in the fridge because I have lost the taste for it. I e-mail my children because I will get more out of the conversation than if they were standing in front of me texting their friends to meet up for a fun evening of watching movies on their big screen TVs.

Looking back I see that the little things that happened in my life, even if it was just an hour or two, developed into the happiest events of my memory. I cannot recreate that time and make it exciting for the family like it was when I was young.

God wants to give you the feeling of excitement and happiness that some enjoy because they are experiencing life with Christ. He wishes it for us, but we have to want this happiness. We have to find our own will or purpose on Earth to find happiness. When we connect with God, not drugs, drink, or other things, He will show us what His will is for our lives. When we submit to God's will I believe happiness follows. The Holy Spirit will fill you with a joy that cannot be discovered with worldly pleasures.

There is no way we can reproduce the joy and excitement that comes with the love God has for us. He wants us to be happy here on earth and when we connect as one with Christ, we begin to feel that joy and love. God has prepared a happiness here on earth. It's up to each individual to ask for God's will to be done. Just as we read in his prayer:

"Thy will be done, on earth as it is in Heaven."

I believe there is a Heaven and that it will truly be a wonderful eternal experience. That is why I look forward to life and life after death. I have seen the divine interventions here on earth and I know there is someone who watches over me.

Someone who loves me even if I am a sinner and mess up every now and then. God is there to pick me up and encourage me to go forward.

We all buy insurance. Why not put your time and effort in the assurance that God gives us on a daily basis. An assurance that he will be there to intervene for his believers.

>John 8:31-32 (NIV)
>*Jesus says, "If you hold to my teaching, you are really my disciples. Then you will know the truth and the truth will set you free."*

Jesus can free us from our sins. Sins can make us slaves to others and things that bring us unhappiness. Jesus promises us that he will free us from our sins and let us be the person God created us to be. Jesus can and will break the power of Sin.

Angels are Ministering Spirits Sent by God to Earth: Listen to Angelic Wisdom

Angels are real and are mentioned several times in the Bible, especially in the New Testament before God sent his son Jesus to come to earth and die for human sin. Have you ever seen an Angel? Do you believe in Angels?

It is obvious, after reading my stories, that I believe that Angels do exist and take charge of my life when I call upon the Lord in times of distress and worry. I also believe that my prayers are important to God because I recognize him as my maker. I am His and He is mine. I have accepted the good and the bad and I look for answers in God's word.

Several years ago before I was married to my husband, my Mother had a heart-attack. I was twenty-eight years old and was living by myself. I had many friends and I had a job making enough money for me to live comfortably. I had a new car, new clothes when I wanted them, and enough money to eat out at least once a week. I had a master's degree and all of my education had been paid. There was no debt except the payment on my apartment. Now that was all any girl could ask for in the '70s.

One thing was missing. I longed for a family of my own. I wanted a husband, children, and a house with a big backyard. I wanted a life that I had dreamed about as a young girl. I didn't grow up with a father's love. Still, I knew that maybe one day, I could find that Prince Charming that would love me unconditionally and life would be just like it was on "Father Knows Best." For those of you too young to remember it was a family show where every family problem was fixed before the end of the show.

As you have already read, I did get my husband I prayed for. What you may not know is that during this time my mother had a serious heart-attack. I remember the family gathering in the hospital waiting for hours for a doctor to come and speak with us concerning her future. He explained that there would not be an operation, and that the heart was dead on one side. He could not promise us anything in writing but hoped that she would respond to some new medication that would be available to heart patients. This new medication will open the small arteries in the healthy side of her heart. This would supply a blood flow to keep her heart and lungs working.

He then said, "If things go well, maybe her life span can be extended for at least four more years. I say four more years but I give no guarantee." Then he left the room and I started to cry.

It was at this time that I realized that I had waited too long to put my life together. I was loosing my mother and she would never be there for me when I found love or when I begin my life as a mother. How could all of this be happening? Why me Lord? I just couldn't imagine being without the one person I wanted to see me be successful. I was already successful, but my definition of the word was having a family of my own. Being able to celebrate holidays with a family just like my siblings. My spirit was crushed. I knew God had already heard me cry out about finding a husband, but could all of this take place in time for my mother to witness my life?

My mother spent a week in ICU. I visited her faithfully everyday. Some days she was aware I was there and some days, she was too weak to talk. I would just sit by her side and quietly watch her breath. She knew how important it was for me to meet the love of my life, but I was her baby and she was never really ready for me to leave home or be away from her.

There was a chapel in the hospital, just like all other hospitals. I walked into that chapel and I started to pray. I called out to God, speaking to him as if he was standing right there in the room with me. I was of course alone, but I asked God to please send me a family so my mother could see me happy before she died. I prayed for her healing. I prayed for the medicine that was going to be the miracle that would give her a few more years of life. I was bowing before God in earnest prayer and pouring out my soul to him for his divine intervention in my life.

After my prayer I walked blurry eyed into the ICU waiting room and asked to see my mother. Then I sat down and waited for the nurse to approve my entrance. To my surprise, she called and asked me if I wanted to come back and feed my mother. I responded with a smile and a loud yes. When I entered her small curtained space, she was sitting up in bed and greeted me with a "Hello Babe."

I fed her some jello and pudding. This was the first she had eaten in days. The nurse said she all of a sudden said she felt better and wanted to eat. Wow, I just knew that God had heard my prayer that day. After several hours of visiting, I went home and my future husband (who was just a voice on the phone) called me and asked me for a date. My friend had given him my number. I asked him to call back. I explained what had happened. I was so week from crying that I could not talk. A week later he called me back and we went out. God was opening up doors and I was not yet aware of how he was working.

The next day when I visited my mother at the hospital, I told her about my phone call. She smiled and told me that she had already heard, from my friend, that he was going to call me and ask me out. I suppose my mother was praying her own little prayer for me.

As weeks passed she continued to gain strength and was able to come home. I on the other hand was dating, my blind date, seriously and sharing everything with my mother. On Easter of that year, Richard met my mother. She had fixed a huge dinner as customary and invited the whole family to dinner. I went to church with him. He came for dinner at my house to meet sisters, cousins, aunts and uncles and about twenty members of our family.

My mother fell in love with him before I did. She told me I was going to marry that guy. I then again did not believe her but knew that God had made me a promise and I hoped that I would soon fall in love and be married before my Mother died.

As the story goes, we did get married the next year and I had two boys. My mother passed up her four year mark and lived for twenty-one years. She was totally in love with her grandchildren. The boys loved her just as much as she loved them.

I know that this was a divine intervention in my life. The doctors were amazed that Mom had made it twenty-one years past her heart-attack. Each doctor visit was a milestone in her life. Her doctor said, "I don't know what you are doing, but just keep doing it." I knew what it was. It was a God thing. He had again answered my prayers and saw that I was truly believing that He was going to supply my needs. Was this a coincidence or a divine intervention?

For me it was a special divine intervention. It convinced me that my God is real and he listens to my prayers. He and only He could answer that earnest prayer I prayed in the hospital chapel.

I met several angels in that hospital while my Mother was recovering. Nurses and nurses aids were there to give her encouragement. People were praying for her daily and ministers from all over Louisville came to see her and pray with her. She believed that she was going to get better. She did fight depression and panic attacks that were delivered by the devil. We had to keep encouraging her to do things. Most of all, we encouraged her to pray and believe that she was going to make it.

My wedding in the fall of the year was a goal that she was trying to obtain. She met a young woman in rehab that she fell in love with. Mom was able to share God's word with her. They remained friends and shared fishing stories. She continued to share her story with believers and nonbelievers. I truly believe that angels watched over her so she could continue to do God's work.

A few days before she died, she saw angels in her room. She had suffered with her heart again and hospitalized for an enlarged heart. It was time for her to go home. She had suffered more attacks and when she felt like she could no longer go on, she was given morphine and fell into a comma. She did not respond to anyone until the day before she died. My boys came to the hospital and held her hand. When they spoke, she opened up her eyes and tried to smile. My children were sure that she knew they were there. My son wrote a poem entitled, "She opened up her eyes." I am sure an angel prompted her to listen in that moment.

She left us in 2003. We felt empty, but we have the assurance that we will again one day meet, and she will see us and know us.

Angels on the Battlefield: A Soldier's Story

Recently I went into a bookstore and on my way out I found the sales table. I could spend a whole day in a bookstore. I not only enjoy reading, I enjoy investigating and learning about History. My hobby is looking up family on Ancestry.com. It is an addiction that many do not understand. I have been reading stories recently written and handed down from grandparents to family members who are crazy, like me, to stay up half the night to see what I missed in the 1800s. If you are interested in this kind of excitement and have wanted to join this web site, beware: you will get hooked.

On the sales table I found a book entitled, "<u>The Haunting of the Presidents</u>." It was written by Joel Martin and William J. Brines. It was a bargain, so I picked it up and headed for the line to pay for my merchandise. When I got home I started to read this book. Immediately I noticed it started talking about angels and divine interventions. "How could this be" I asked myself? Then I started to read.

The civil war was a horrific battle that smelled of death and left tons of men dying for what they passionately believed in. The freedom of America would never be cultivated for our generation if these brave soldiers had not given up their lives. Every solider that died in this battle was destined to give up life so I and my children could live in a free country. God knew each soldier and had a plan for each man before he was born. He knew which soldier that would take the bullet for me and my generation. He consoled the families that lost love ones. He provided spouses to widows that could not make it on their own. He surrounded the men with comfort from angels before they died. He gave strength and guidance to those who made it through the war. I am convinced that God was there the whole way. He knew what had to happen to make America a free and holy place to worship.

I am also convinced that without pain nothing can be born, developed, or made. We see this in childbirth. We see it when we have an operation to heal the body. We see it with our young children when we send them off to school for the first time only to have them come home crying that they miss the comfort of home and their family. As time passes the child understands that school is not going away. It is a way of life and the tears leave as they battle for attention from teachers and classmates. They also learn that the award is given at the end of twelve years and lessons learned in school were necessary. The pain of accomplishments grows strength and guidance that help us to endure life.

The most important place we notice "good" coming from "pain" is Christ dying on the cross. What pain he endured that day. He was obedient to God and He knew that this had to happen to save us from our sins. With His death He gave us grace and forgiveness knowing that we are sinners and we desire to be like Christ, but being in a sinful world it is not possible to remain obedient without God's grace.

This book reminisced the stories of George Washington and the battle he endured at Valley Forge and Gettysburg. The winter was one of the coldest winters that has ever existed in history. The men were unclothed, unfed, and unpaid. They marched relentlessly over hills and through icy water to obey the commands of their leader, George Washington. The wind pushed the freezing rain through the skin of the soldiers like nails being driven through an unfinished roof. Some of the men were suffering from frostbite. The toes in their shoes were broken because of the brittle rocks that sliced through the leather. Socks were wet and bare legs were hanging from scraps of material that were torn from the pants that once protected their body from the conditions of the weather. Gun shots could be heard from the British army who was gaining ground behind the suffering American troops. Soldiers who could not keep the marching pace lagged behind and were captured by the enemy.

The area where the soldiers were to stop for the night to gather fresh clothes, food, and water was barren. The troops had planned to requisition adequate supplies, warm themselves, and secure quarters in a secret thicket, but the ground was frozen and the wagon wheels could not roll along the ground. The general's tent had been pitched before the weather moved into the area and a guard was stationed outside. It could not hold the whole troop. Washington being the man of concern who loved his men, shared his tent and took turns gathering in the huddle with his troops to keep warm. He wanted to share in all the inconvenience that his troop had to endure.

Desperately, Washington wrote congress and asked for help. He even complained to the Board of War, but there were several people who were true to England and did not support the war. Funds for the war effort were slim and board members were objecting to Washington's effort.

George Washington was ready to dispatch his troops and give up. He had been praying every step of the way asking the Lord to watch over his troops and keep their sprits high. As he walked into his quarters and sat down at a small desk to write his dispatch paper, an Angel appeared to him. He did not see it come into his space and he had never seen this person before. He told the person that he had given strict orders not to be disturbed. Still the visitor did not move.

Washington was so astonished that he could not speak. He watched as the vision spoke to him. He was told that America was under the control of God. A vision of the world was on a map that was laid before him and he could see America springing up with villages and towns. Then Washington saw an American flag between the countries on the map. A vision of soldiers putting down their guns and the voice said, "Remember, we are brothers. The whole world united shall not prevail against her." The last words of wisdoms Washington heard were, "Let every child of the Republic learn to live for his God, his land, and his Union."

There was much more to this meeting that gave Washington a vision of wars that may lie ahead for America. With each war there was victory. Washington renewed the faith he needed. He could see that America could gain freedom. He was certain that the message he was given meant that he would have victory over the British. When he left the tent there stood before him his men who had rallied to finish the war and emerge stronger on the British.

Soon the weather changed and help came to America from two military experts from Europe. They brought troops, supplies and a strong fighting force. Together they won the battle and claimed victory over the British. All hostilities were ended and this became a huge victory for George Washington. He believed that his faith in God had sent him an angel to protect and encourage him as a General to keep the faith and fight for the freedom of his country.

George Washington never spoke about that night until much later. He shared his story with his close friend and young aid Anthony Sherman who many years later shared it with a reporter who wrote about it in the *National Tribune* in 1880. It is the agreement of all who have been troubled with hopeless situations throughout the centuries that God guides humanity and plans its destiny.

It is often written home in letters that soldiers on the battlefield experience protective angels who encourage and provide comfort to young men whose lives were in harms way. Has a divine intervention been responsible for George Washington's victory at Valley Forge? I believe it had a great affect on him as a believer and a General in command of failing troops who were ready to give up life and breath to stop the fighting. That same spirit that spoke with Washington also gave hope to his troops. How else could they have been revived and encouraged to continue?

On December 4, 1783, General Washington met with his men for the last time. He gave them a speech that I am sure all remembered. "While we are zealously performing the duties of good citizens and soldiers, we certainly ought not to be inattentive to the higher duties of religion."

In other speeches Washington showed signs of his devotion to America and linked them to the protection of freedom to worship. This story sums up my belief of divine intervention. God's plan for each of us, to be who we were designed to be. Each one of us special in our own way. Read God's word and notice that the Old Testament had a long history of foretelling the future of the coming events. When these events were given to prophets they became real to the people. God's word was alive. The people started to listen and believe.

Today Jesus Christ remains the most gifted of all prophets. We will never know how many times he will send angels to help us. People who are strangers and are aware of our needs may be sent from God.

1 Timothy 3:16
Beyond all question the mystery of godliness is great:

He appeared in a body, was vindicated by the Spirit, was seen by angels, was preached among the nations, was believed on in the world, was taken up in glory. (NIV)

God is faithful to his people and if he promises us that he will protect us and give us life everlasting, I believe him.

2 Timothy 2:12
If we endure, we will also reign with him, if we disown him, he will also disown us.

It is known that demons live in this world. They control wickedness and influence human beings. Evil spirits dwell in those who are not believers. The Bible speaks of demonic forces and dark forces. He speaks of demon angels that are cast into darkness to be judged.

If God does not spare the angels who sinned, but cast them into hell, then I am sure he is very serious about his children who do not believe in Christ or glorify Him.

Let the Spiritual Forces be Acknowledged: The Trip

In 1970 our family bought a new RV. It had all the newest convinces of home. It was large enough to sleep seven but with a few foam mats, we squeezed in ten. We were taking a trip out west and it would be a trip of a lifetime. We visited the Grand Canyon, Old Faithful, and all the points of interest in-between. I had invited a friend and my uncle was delivering two nephews back to their home in Kansas. This is why we ended up with three extra family members on board.

The week before the trip we were buying groceries and packing clothes in the camper. I walked into the camper carrying some towels and dishes when I stopped and sat down on the couch. There was something about that camper that was making me feel very uncomfortable. I was excited about the trip from the beginning and knowing that my best friend was going to experience the trip with me was an extra plus. I ignored the feeling and continued to pack and cram snacks and clothes into the spaces above the couch bed.

The next day, as I continued to pack my clothes along with my mother, I had the same feeling of unrest. Everything I looked at made my head swim and I started to feel dizzy and sick. I could feel a dark force over me. Instead of feeling excited about the trip, I was beginning to feel anxious about the trip. I turned to my mother and asked her if she could smell something strange in the camper. She said that she thought it was the newness of the leather on the seats. It was not what I was smelling. I couldn't explain what was making me dizzy or why I dreaded being in that camper.

As the days passed I would continue to enter the camper and walk around looking in storage bins and trying out chairs and beds. Still, I felt very uncomfortable in there. My heart was beating hard and I just couldn't explain why. I was almost ready to back out of the trip. This was a trip of a lifetime and I just couldn't figure out what was going on in my head. I mentioned it to my mother and she passed it off as being nervous about leaving home and my sister.

I couldn't explain the feeling to her. It was something that had to be experienced. I was becoming obsessed with leaving in that van. I asked mom again if she would just listen to me and understand that I had a bad feeling about the trip. She told me if I felt that strong about the trip that I should pray about it. I agreed that if I felt that uncomfortable that I should ask God to comfort me. That night I found my small white Bible and packed it in with my clothes. I prayed and prayed all the time that God would protect us and let everything be okay with the van. I prayed for safety constantly.

The day we left, I went out and found my seat along with the other members of the family. Everyone was so excited. We played cards, sang, read books, and that night we pulled into an RV park and found our place in the van to sleep. Before I went to sleep I again prayed asking God to protect us as we traveled. We had a long way to go before we got into Kansas. That was our first stop: to deliver the two boys. The next morning I remember it being extremely hot. We ate breakfast and couldn't wait to get back in the air conditioned van. The Boys were young and they were getting on our nerves so we were looking forward to getting them home. The others played games with the boys and I started to feel uncomfortable so I got my Bible out of my space and started to read. I wish I could remember what I read, but I can't. I just know that I was quietly praying and asking God to watch over us and keep us safe.

We were looking for a place to eat lunch, but we were in the middle of nowhere. Nothing but wheat fields and flat dry land. We were just a few hours before we would be in the city so snacking was on the menu. We were all getting tired and some had decided to take a nap. It was about 3 in the afternoon and all of a sudden the Van started shaking back and forth. My uncle and step father started to get excited.

"Do we have a flat tire?" asked my mom.

The men screamed, "Maybe more than one."

We were flopping from side to side and things were falling out of the cabinets. We ducked under the shelves trying to hold on to the sides of the wall. The van leaned on two wheels as my step father directed it toward the side of the road. Fortunately the van seemed to be stable as the men opened up the door and saw that two tires were off – one in the front and one in back. Carefully, each one of us walked slowly toward the door as the van teetered back and forth. When the door was shut the van bumped down and leaned against the ditch. The door was pushed up against the dirt and could not be opened.

The men ran down the road and recovered the wheels. Both tires seemed to be in good shape. Now it was becoming a mystery. Did we hit something in the road? The drivers said they saw nothing in the road. It was like an earthquake. The wheels just started to come off.

We all sat on the side of the road in the heat that was close to 90 degrees. The bugs were biting and we were tired and hungry. We waited for at least an hour before the problem was discovered. The van had lost its lug bolts that held on the huge tires. Without the lug bolts there was no way to put the tires back on. Realizing we were on a long lonely road and few cars were passing us we all began to panic. This was a time before cell phones so there was no way to call for help. The best we could hope for was a trucker with a radio. After several hours, a trucker came by and stopped to help us. He took the men to the next filling station where they were able to find a tow truck to pull the van out of the ditch. It was now dark and we were all still sitting on the side of the road waiting for the guys to come back and pick us up.

I was silently praying. God had sent his angels to guide the van carefully to the side of the road and stabilized it long enough for us to get out. It was a miracle that we were not killed. The two remaining tires were the only thing that kept us from turning over. The van stayed in the service station for two days on cinder blocks. The closest Ford dealer was two days away and the lug bolts had to come from the dealer. We were able to stay in the camper but we could not have any air or electric for cooking.

Fortunately there was a small country kitchen in the service station and we ate all of our meals there. We stayed in that field for two and a half days. We would sit on the picnic table out in front of the restaurant. Fortunately the table was in the shade and we could catch a breeze now and then. I knew that God was in this event. I had prayed so much for safety that I am sure he had sent his angels to gently glide us to the side of the road so we were not hurt in any way. A truck had to bring the parts to us from a town in Kansas. Each day we would watch for a truck to come pass the station. Eagerly we would cross our fingers and pray that this would be the one.

The two younger boys were now getting on everyone's nerves. My aunt and Mom were trying hard to be patient, but lost their temper several times as the boys ran in and out of the camper eating the few snacks we had stored.

When we finally got the van up and running, and we were back on the road, my mom looked at me and said, "Do you feel any better about this trip?"

I replied, "It's going to be all right now. Let's just get these boys home."

It was all right and we had a wonderful trip after our two day stop right outside of no where. I will never forget that trip and I will never forget the feeling that I had before we had the accident. It was so clear to me that I had to pray for safety. God had my attention and I was asking him to send his angels to protect us. I believe that this was a divine intervention. I also believe that we should always ask for protection when we travel. God is always there and he does hear your prayers and concerns.

Don't be Reluctant to Listen to God: Have Faith and Obey

Mike had just met the love of his life. He was a young man with a wild spirit. He had done it all. Drugs, alcohol, and motorcycle gangs led him to a group of men and women who were sharing free sex and love. He didn't believe in God and he didn't believe that stuff about church and going to heaven. He married his girl and looked forward to the weekends to ride and romp all over the city. His language was raw to say the least and taking God's name in vain was never an issue.

Tina was sexually and verbally abused as a teenager. She longed for the weekend to travel with her boyfriend Mike. She made it to her senior year and quit school to follow her heart. She wasn't interested in working or finding a career. Her main goal was to get away from her step father and mother. She would live with her new husband in the basement of his father's house. She never thought about having a home or a family. She wasn't use to being loved and cared for. The only love she knew was the attention that Mike occasionally gave her when he was happy and high.

Mike had a job working in a factory. On Mondays he would have a hard time going to work because of the hangover that lingered in the air from the weekend parties. Day after day he would come home and drink a few beers and fall asleep on the couch. Mike's father was also an alcoholic. He was not surprised that Mike was following in his footsteps. He hated it but expected Mike was just going to be like him. This is the life that he had taken on since he was in his late twenties. Mike's mother had left him after fifteen years of marriage. When Mike became seventeen he left the comfort of home to live with his father.

Mike and Tina lived in that basement for a year. Tina got a job as a waitress and together they figured that it was enough to pay for their weekend parties. Sleeping on the run and saving enough money for gas and beer.

When Mike was sharing this story with me he did not want to tell me all the details. I am sure he was embarrassed to admit how much time and effort he had put into partying and destroying his body. Tina was so in love with Mike that she would do just about anything to make him happy. The motorcycle group they belonged to was the only family the young couple knew. It was the safe place from those who did not accept their lifestyle.

Mike said an accident was a wake-up call for him. He had been riding on an expressway when a car crossed the line and flipped his cycle and it landed in a pile of trees and logs along side the road. He said he did not remember how long he laid there but when he came to, he was in a hospital room and on life support. Tina was expecting their first child and she was consumed with worry.

"How could this be happening to us" she asked

"We have been through so much, why this?" she questioned.

Mike stayed in the ICU for several days. A minister came in to visit with him. He encouraged Mike and asked if he could pray for him. Mike agreed. He then told Mike that he would be back to see him the next day.

As promised, the minister made his rounds and made sure that he stopped to see Mike. Again he prayed for Mike and promised to return. The next time the minister visited, Mike was off the breathing tube and could speak. He was able to share with the minister what had happened and ask if he could get in touch with his wife, Tina. He promised he would. Then he asked Mike if he attended any church. Mike said no, and then told him that he didn't believe in God. The Minister was able to share God's word with Him and promised that when he visits his members in the hospital, he will stop by again. When the minister walked out of the room he shoved Tina's phone number into his pocket and said he would call Tina and share Mike's progress.

Mike had time to lay there and think. What was he going to do with his life? He had to work. He had to get better to help Tina take care of the baby. Everything was coming so quick. Maybe this minister was right. He had to change his lifestyle. He didn't want to give up his bike, but it would give him money for the baby.

Soon Mike and the minister were friends. He had met Tina and he continued to share the word with both of them. He bought them Bibles and when Mike was well enough to leave the hospital, Mike promised the minister he would attend his church.

I am not quit sure what happened from here, but Mike was so excited telling me about his Christian life that he skipped most of his story. He and Tina have a son and a daughter. He was wild about sharing his connection to God. He was so full of the Holy Spirit that he was talking fast and moving all around the room. He accepted the Lord as his savior and since be became a Christian, he has never touched another drop of liquor or drugs. God healed his body and together he and Tina witness to youth in the church.

"I have a story to tell," said Mike.

"I let God into every inch of my life."

"I can talk to God and I know he listens, because he will give me messages to do certain things."

"Can you tell me about that?" I asked.

"Yes, I was working in the factory and not making enough money to keep us afloat. I didn't want to quit my job, because you know it is so hard to find work these days."

"I understand," I replied.

"I shared this with Tina and we started praying about a new job. Then one day I ran into a guy that I went to school with. He was talking about this awesome job where he was working for a construction company. He told me how much he made and it was twice what I was making at my job."

"Before I could ask if they were hiring, he said, 'You know they are hiring there and they have wonderful benefits. You should check it out."

He gave me the address and I went over to the company and filled out an application. I was sure that this was the answer to my prayers. The next day I got up started to go to work and something just told me to wait. I never miss work, but there was such a strong push for me to go and hang out at my thinking place near the river. I drove over there, got out of my truck and started walking and praying. I was asking God what I should do. I walked passed a young mother, grandmother, and little boy. I politely spoke and noticed that the mother had tears in her eyes.

"Are you okay?" I asked.

"Well, sir I am loosing my husband to cancer and we have not told my son yet."

"We thought we would bring him to the playground and talk to him," said the young woman.

"He is just five years old and I really don't know what to say. I can't stop crying long enough to have the conversation."

Mike turned to the mother and asked her if she was a Christian. She replied with a no. Then Mike started to witness to her about God and Heaven. He got his Bible out of the truck and read several verses to the young girl and her mother. He explained that there was a Heaven and that he knew for certain that he was going to go there when he died. He spent over an hour witnessing to the two women. The young boy playing in the distance got tired of the slide and came running to the picnic table. The mother introduced the boy to her new friend.

"This man was telling us a story about a man named Jesus."

The boy looked puzzled and noticed that both of the women were crying. Without another word, Mike asked the boy to sit by his side. Then he showed him the Bible.

"You see son, there was this man who loves us so much that he wants us to come and live with him someday. His name is Jesus. We know him because he left us stories in this book I have," replied Mike.

Then Mike started to tell him that someday every one of us are going to visit that man in Heaven. He explained Heaven and what he believed it must look like. Then Mike told him that his grandfather and grandmother were in Heaven and he planned to visit them someday after he died.

Mike told me that it seemed that God was putting the words in his mouth. He was able to talk about sick people and how some get well and some don't get well. He told me that they talked about the little boy's father being sick and that maybe he would not be staying here but may be visiting Heaven. Mike had quite a story to tell the young boy. When he finished the story his mother and grandmother were consoled that the little boy had learned about death in a special way.

Then Mike told me that he left the park and went home. As he walked in the door the phone was ringing and it was the construction company offering him a job.

"You see how God works?" said Mike.

"I listened to that small voice in my spirit that day and I just could not go to work."

"I believe God wanted to use me to tell this little boy about his father's cancer. When I did what God had in store for me, I think he listened to my prayers and knew that this job was important to me and my family."

"So you think God used you as one of his earthly angels?" I asked.

"I am not sure, but I do know that two women were saved that day and I have checked up on them," said Mike.

"Are they believers now?" I asked.

"They are attending church and the father is still sick but alive, living with cancer," said Mike.

"What about your job?" I asked.

"I love it, and I thank God every day for that job," said Mike.

I am not sure that Mike has ever seen an angel but I am certain that he has a special relationship with God that gives him a spiritual awakening and encourages him to stop and share his faith with others. Mike also knows that he not only desires God, but that he desires to share his faith with every one he meets.

This divine intervention was a special delivery message from God. Mike had no idea that God had planned for him to share his faith with strangers that day. He never missed work and didn't plan to miss work as he drove his truck past the park and the river. He was earnestly in prayer and listening to his spirit. In the end there was a blessing for all involved.

Follow the Light While Walking Through the Battlefields of Life

When you believe that God can and will send help in a divine intervention then you have discovered the light in your life. The Bible refers to Jesus as the Light! When we open our minds and heart and accept God as our father and protector, we see He has the power to change lives.

God is always in control and it is only through Him that we can stand on the battlefield of life without giving up. We will have battles and strife in life. God tells us that there will be times of failure and disappointment. He also tells us that in these times we should look to Him to help us solve our problems.

> Job 28:12-13
> *Where can wisdom be found? Where does understanding dwell? Man does not comprehend its worth; it cannot be found in the land of the living.*

Once you become intimate with God, you will understand how much he loves you and wants to protect you. You will hunger for his word. You will pray to him and talk to him as if he is your best friend. He will light your pathway and show you where you should and should not tread.

> Psalm 91:9-15
> *If you make the Most High your dwelling – then no harm will befall you. For he will command his angels' concerning you to guard you in all your ways; so that you will not strike your foot against a stone. You will tread upon the lion and the serpent. Because he loves me, "Says the Lord, I will rescue him; I will protect him, for he acknowledges my*

> *name." He will call upon me, and I will answer him; I will be with him in trouble, I will deliver him and honor him.*

This is positive proof that there is a divine intervention when we call upon the Lord.

> Matthew 28:20
> *Jesus says, "Lo I am with you always, even to the end of the age."*

This is the promise of protection from God. God has made you special because you have made him a part of your life. Call upon his name in times of trouble. He will intervene if you have faith and believe.

Recently we have had our share of rain. It has rained 20 inches this spring and the Ohio River is covering the road and closing nearby businesses and homes. Events and ball games have been rained out and everyone is praying for the sunshine. Homes are sandbagging their foundations and people have seen all kinds of destruction in small towns from Tennessee to Florida. Homes were hit by tornadoes and destroyed. Watching the news I saw families who lost their homes but gave thanks to God for saving their lives. They are saying it was a miracle that we are all alive.

My family and I were eating at a restaurant when the rain poured out of the sky. It was raining so fast that we could not see the cars in the parking lot. Enjoying our food we decided to take our time to visit and eat. When the rain stopped, I noticed that people were gathering around the door. As we walked out the door and looked to the sky, we saw a double rainbow that covered the entire space around the restaurant. There is no word to describe the beauty that we witnessed that evening. It was God's promise to the people. In Genesis 9:18 God promised us a rainbow as a covenant between the animals and the living people that he would never destroy the world again by water. There was the proof right in front of us. Why then should we not believe him when he tells us that he will provide safety and protection?

Reading the word has convinced me that nothing is by chance. There is a higher being that guides us and knows us personally. I have also learned that it is important to share your experience with others. It doesn't matter if someone doubts you, just remember that God knows the truth and sharing your divine interventions can prove that God is real and he does intervene in our lives to protect us from evil. The events in life happen for a reason and being aware of the interventions help you to connect to your purpose in life.

A Brain Tumor

It was June 18, and my husband and I had just returned from our trip to Orange Beach. It was a good trip, but I remember asking my husband if he thought the sun was extremely bright.

"It's always hot and bright in June," he replied.

I had tried to polish my nails on the balcony and could not see where my nail started or ended. I had polish all over my fingers. I again blamed it on the bright sun. My sister and husband laughed at me as they watched me trying to take the polish back off of my fingers.

We drove home after a week and I remember sleeping most of the way home. I had finished this book and was looking forward to sending it to my editor. My husband and I stopped to eat and I took out my calendar to see what was in store for us when we returned home. My husband looked at me and asked if I had put his surgery on my calendar.

"When is your surgery, honey?" I asked.

"The 14th of June," he replied.

"That's day after tomorrow," I explained.

I knew that my husband had planned on having sinus surgery sometime in the summer but I had not put it on my calendar. Here we go, not even back in Kentucky and our schedule is about to get clogged up again.

When we arrived home, there was a message for Rich on the answering machine telling him how to prepare for his surgery.

We gathered all the necessary papers and headed for the outpatient surgery center on Tuesday morning. It was a five-hour surgery. I remember trying to read in the waiting room but it just seemed to dark. I picked up my purse and book and headed outside to a bench in front of the building. When the surgery was over the doctor came looking for me and found me sitting outdoors. He told me to get his medicine and some four by four squares to pack his nose.

I brought Rich home and gave him his pain medication. Then I tried to follow him to the bathroom to pad his bleeding nose. At this point I fell and hit my foot on the kitchen stool. It hurt so much, but I was trying to be brave. I didn't want Rich to know how much I was hurting.

It was a long night for both of us, but we made it to the next morning. I had a doctor's appointment for a check-up and so I left Rich in bed with all the necessary equipment needed to get him through the morning. I limped out the door to the thirty-mile doctor's visit in Prospect, Kentucky. My foot was killing me. My doctor noticed the limp and sent me to the ER to get an ex-ray. He followed up with the ER and told me I had chipped my foot and broken my toe. I needed to get the x-ray and see the orthopedic doctor soon.

I drove home in a rainstorm and could hardly see where I was going. I returned to my job as a nurse and told my husband that I had broken my foot. He was still packed with gauze and on pain medicine. I waited until Friday to make an appointment with the foot doctor. I had to take Rich back to the doctor to get his packing out and they wanted him to take two pain pills before his appointment. While helping him in the car, I noticed that I could not see well. I closed my right eye and I could not see at all out of my left eye.

"What next?" I thought. I can't tell him I can't see out of my left eye. I drove him to the doctor and sat there trying to close my eye and read a flyer on the table in the waiting room. It only confirmed that something was wrong with my left eye. I took Rich home and put him to bed. Then I went to Bizer's Vision World where my son worked, and asked to have my eyes examined.

"It's packed right now, mom," replied my son. "Can you come back at five thirty?"

I agreed to return at five thirty and Byron, my son, got me right back to see one of the doctors. The doctor gave me several eye exams. I flunked all of them. Then he told me that he felt that I had a tumor that was blocking the sight in my left eye. I was in shock.

Right there he called the eye surgeon and asked him to see me on Saturday morning. He explained that it was an emergency. Now Byron and I were both worried.

On Saturday I left Rich and asked my son to check in on his dad. My sister took me to the surgeon's office. He opened his office just for me. Again, he gave me all kinds of eye tests and again I flunked them all.

"Mrs. K you need to get an MRI tonight. Right away, and I don't care where you get one," he explained. "I think you have a tumor on your pituitary gland," he continued.

My sister took me to the hospital and I had an MRI that night. As we expected, the doctor was right. There was a huge tumor on my pituitary gland and it was putting pressure on the nerve of my left eye. The Emergency Room doctor called my neural surgeon and had me see him on Monday. Everything was going so quickly.

By ten o'clock that night one of my close friends had heard the news and it spread like wildfire. There were seven people at the hospital praying for me before I could get home and give Rich the good news.

The next week I went to the hospital for test and met with an ENT who would assist with the surgery. Surgery was set for Saturday.

"It must be important to get this removed if the surgeons are coming in on Saturday," said my nurse friend who worked at the hospital.

I had several people coming to my house to pray with me. People everywhere were praying for a successful surgery. I went into the hospital on Saturday morning, and I was sure that God was going to take care of my problem. If things didn't work out I also knew that I was ready to meet my Maker. It would be okay for me any way it went.

I spent two nights in ICU and three days in the hospital. My nose was broken and packed. I also had swollen cheeks and bruising all over my face. I was a mess to see. It took lots of rest and several weeks to get back to looking like myself.

When the operation was finished, I looked at the crowd of friends standing in the hall and covered my right eye.

"I can see out of my left eye," I screamed.

Everyone clapped.

The tumor was huge and had broken apart. No wonder the doctors were worried. It had been there for a long time. I was lucky that the doctors were there to do the surgery right away.

Weeks later when I went back to the eye surgeon, he examined my eyes and told me I had 20/20 vision. He then explained that vision usually does not come back all the way.

"I can't believe your vision is so good," he explained.

I could see tears coming down his cheeks.

I begin to cry and so did the assistant and my husband.

"It's a miracle," said the doctor. "A miracle," he said again.

As we left the room crying the office person saw all of us and asked what happened in the small examining room.

"They're tears of joy," said the assistant.

Looking back, I can understand that I fell because I could not see out of my left eye. Four weeks later I fell again and made another trip to the ER where I had four stitches in my toe sewed up. Now the doctors had to address the break on my left foot. I wore a cast the rest of the summer. Again if I had not fallen, the break on my foot would not have been addressed. You see sometimes a divine intervention is not always what we expect.

I do know that God was in control of my operation and he was with the surgeons and doctors who took care of me.

I am writing this story in January of 2012 and my book has been with the publisher for many months. It was important to list one more event where a divine intervention saved my life. I hope you now believe in miracles and the power of prayer.

Afterword

I hope you have enjoyed reading the stories that were shared in this book. Writing about personal events can sometimes be emotionally draining. I know God has been present as I have shared my life events. I have often said to people that I should not have been born. My parents were older. They had been married fourteen years before I was born. My parents were also in the middle of a separation and eventually divorced. Still God knew that I was to be born and he knew me and had a purpose for my life as I developed in my mother's womb. I hope you will share this book with your friends or use it as a study guide in your book club. My hope for you is to recognize your divine interventions and log them.

May God bless you and give you the peace you deserve as one of his children.

How Do We Define Divine Interventions?

Group Discussion:

1   Miracles from God

2   Unexplained events

3   Guided by angels

4   Faithfulness given by God

5   Changes in life's pathway

Log Your Divine Interventions

I.

II.

III.

About the Author

LS King is a native of Louisville, Kentucky. She graduated from University of Louisville where she earned a masters degree in education. Mrs. King loves to write true stories about phenomenal people and events. Her first two books, *No Ordinary Woman* and *Lady Bray* are examples of strong women who overcame adversity at the turn of the 20th Century. The books are not only entertaining but paint a historical view of the time the characters grew up in.

Her books also reflect her strong faith in God, with the new book *Divine Interventions* portraying actual events that happened in Mrs. King's life and the lives of people she knows. From graduating college, to teaching school, to being nominated as one of Louisville's phenomenal women in 2001, Mrs. King hopes her books will be an inspiration and blessing to all who read them.

Also from BlackWyrm...

No Ordinary Woman
by LS King

This factual diary of Violet Beanblossom takes the reader from events in the 1900s and follows her life until her death in 2003. Violet not only overcame adversity, but became a successful businesswoman, owning her own business as early as 1959. She became one of the first daycare owners in Louisville. The story will tug at your heartstrings as she records her painful life experiences.

The Misadventures of a Country Girl
by Teddi Robinson

This is the true story of the author growing up in Harrison County, Indiana. Her adventures include the 1937 flood, a sixty-foot deep cave, a snake den, and other escapades that an exploring city child can find in the country.

www.blackwyrm.com

www.ingramcontent.com/pod-product-compliance
Lightning Source LLC
Chambersburg PA
CBHW061445040426
42450CB00007B/1221